40 Maths Games to Make and Play

The Early Years

Margaret Williams
and
Heather Somerwill

M
MACMILLAN

First published 1982
Reprinted 1983, 1984, 1988, 1989

Published by
MACMILLAN EDUCATION LTD
Houndmills, Basingstoke, Hampshire RG21 2XS
and London
Companies and representatives
throughout the world

Design and artwork by Tek-Art
Croydon, Surrey

Printed in Hong Kong

ISBN 0-333-31730-0

Contents

Part 1

Part 2

Part 1

Introduction

This book is the culmination of many years work with young children in the classroom. We began working together after both being members of a teachers' centre group devising mathematical apparatus for use in the classroom. We quickly realised that there was little commercial apparatus tailored for our requirements and so we began making simple games to meet individual needs in our classrooms. We found that the children really enjoyed our games and eagerly awaited new ones. They seemed to appreciate that we were making these games especially for them and therefore looked after the materials. At the same time we realised that the children were doing more calculations in their heads as a result of the games than they could possibly do on paper.

The full potential of these activities was soon apparent, particularly with children entering school who were not ready for the more formal aspects of work. It is a commonly held belief that before children can undertake writing and the use of symbols they need many structured play activities which will lead to an understanding of early number and these games provided the required structured play. In this way children can be doing mathematics before they are ready to read and write and they can have basic number concepts before they are able to record them. The games therefore became a means of introducing and practising new concepts which is why matching activities and cardinal numbers feature significantly in our first section of games.

We then devised games which catered for the older children in vertically grouped classes, such as counting on and addition and subtraction games. Over the years the section for older children has been developed and elaborated in response to requests from colleagues who have used this games approach successfully. Some of the games which need adult supervision enabled us to utilise the valuable resource of mother helpers. We encouraged the mothers to watch us introduce the games to the children so that they not only learn how to play the games but could also understand the teaching points. By using these games within the integrated day we found that we had more teaching time available for other group activities knowing that all the children were practising number skills in a meaningful way.

Why play games?

Children enjoy playing games. They play for excitement, for challenge and for relief from boredom. Whilst playing games children are relaxed and have a good learning disposition. Games which become familiar and loved help create a confident and secure atmosphere in the classroom and may even bring the isolated child into social interaction with other children.

Children gain security in their environment through knowledge of the rules of the society in which they find themselves. Sometimes these rules are rather negative, for instance, 'Don't walk on the grass' 'Don't make so much noise in the canteen'. Through using these games children come to understand that rules have a necessary function and can bring enjoyment and success and are not always an outside imposition. They learn about mathematics in the real world and that learning tables has a real purpose. With careful structure, games can make repetitive memorising interesting, give children practice in learning number facts, create new learning situations and reinforce lightly held knowledge.

They also provide other advantages, such as sharing, which is an important aspect of a child's social training and language is developed as games become integrated into the infant curriculum. Manipulative skills are also acquired through handling the 'playwiths' and lastly, or should it be firstly they are developing linguistic skills through new experiences and situations. An important facet of all the games is the language used by the children or drawn from them by questioning.

Mathematical development

Our first games were tailored to meet the requirements of our own children but as time went on and our collection of games grew, we began to realise that the games were covering the development of mathematics. It was then that we decided to look at number to see if our games covered each aspect. Requests from our Mathematics Adviser to talk at Teachers' Centres in Devon about our games, inspired us to make more games with a child's growth in number knowledge in mind.
The main objectives that we agreed were necessary in the early years number programme were practice in matching and sorting, cardinality of number, and the understanding through ordinality, of whole numbers and their relationship with one another. Counting on games provide the necessary practice leading to an understanding of the number line.

Measurement and shopping were practical exercises in our classrooms and we never felt the need to make games for these areas of the mathematics curriculum. Aspects of weight emerged from cooking and with the younger children we used a balancing and ratio approach, for example, two eggs balancing the margarine, then the sugar and finally the flour. As the children got older and understood the standard unit of a kilogram, we used grams. Before cooking, the children visited a cake shop to see how cakes were marketed. On their return to school they created their own shopping situations selling their cakes. Shopping was therefore seen as a real activity with real money, goods and value, for which games are no substitute. Our children also had real shopping experiences selling crisps and apples at morning break. Selling real things overcame the problem of making the playshop realistic and mathematically correct.

The facility of using standard measures of length arose from comparing lengths of ribbons, objects and toys such as long furry animals and then the use of a standard arbitrary unit. Again, because of the practical nature of these activities, games were not necessary. Volume and capacity activities with sand and water trays were also practical.

In group situations an awareness of time was constantly being taught, as the conceptual language in the early stages is so difficult to learn. As time is cyclic in nature we made dials to portray the days of the week and months of the year. Reading the clock face was taught by using real clocks and watches. The games which we found were most successful and valuable therefore, were those dealing with number. A lot of practice is needed and games provided the variety needed to give adequate practice and still sustain the children's interest.

When do we play games?

The modern infant classroom gives opportunities for games to be played at any time of the day. Games are fun and children enjoy playing them, but our games were also an important part of the curriculum and took their place alongside the other mathematical activities that we planned. We used games to introduce concepts and to reinforce them. In our vertically grouped classes we had the advantage of an older child playing with a younger one, where the older child was perhaps reinforcing a known concept and the younger child was learning a new one.

We found that the best way to introduce a new game was to have a large group sitting on the floor playing the game with us. Once the children knew how to play a game we found that two players were enough, unless of course they were being supervised. However games lend themselves to use in many ways. We feel it is important to view the games as part of the curriculum, to be used to meet specific needs within the classroom. It is important not to relegate the games to wet Friday afternoons or as a special treat, i.e. to fill in time.

Games need to be played within the mathematics context either after a new skill has been taught, as a follow up activity or used as an introduction to a new skill. Hopefully the enthusiasm and good learning disposition children brng to the playing of games will come to be associated with mathematics.

Making the games

As all the games are board games we always use thick card as it lasts longer, and cover it with a self-adhesive plastic film, which not only lengthens the life of the game but helps retain its appearance. Dirt can easily be removed with soap and water or nail varnish remover. Not being artistic, we use pictures cut from mail order catalogues, discarded library books, magazines, scraps and gift wrapping paper to illustrate the games. When the game is illustrated and covered we put two holes at one edge, with reinforcing eyelets, and then thread string through the holes.

The traditional counters used in most commercial games were very difficult for little fingers to manipulate and so we use small cowboys, lorries, animals etc which can be bought or made with felt. They have far more appeal and also add to the individuality of the game. Commercial dice are not always satisfactory as they are too small and do not have the variety of numbers on them that are needed. We made our own from foam. We cut blocks from thick foam $6cm^3$. They were covered with felt, hand stitched around the edges with numerals either embroidered or stuck on.

The requirements of the dice were different for each game so we made one for each game.

The size of the boards given in Part 2 of this book are approximate only and were in fact the size of the originals which suited the needs of the games at that time. The size is by no means obligatory and when making the game the size of the board used will depend on the illustrations to be used, the space available for storing the games, the number of children to play and the place where it is to be played.

Storing and coding the games

Once we had accumulated several games we found two problems arose. One was storing the games which were not needed for immediate use, and the other was making the games freely available to the children complete with dice and counters. The first problem was overcome by using a paper storage cabinet, each tray holding games of different levels. Stored centrally, the games were available to all the teachers in the school and they could also add their own games.

The games currently in use were hung from cup hooks in the classroom.

Each game was accompanied by a coded bag which contained the necessary dice and counters. Parents made these miniature shoe bags from remnants of material and then a scrap of the material was stuck on the back of the game so that the bag matched the game. Alternatively we embroidered a simple picture on the bag which corresponded with a picture on the board. The children were therefore able to check whether they had the right bag for the game they were playing.

Our reading books had been colour coded to determine their readability level and we transferred this method of coding to our maths games. Early matching and sorting games had a red sticker which matched a hook on the wall from which those early games hung. Yellow spots were used for cardinal number games and green for counting on games. Children were then easily directed to those games which suited their level of achievement in mathematics.

Rules

We found that it was important to have rules for each of the games written on the back of the boards. The rules were carefully printed in language easily understood by the children and they were encouraged to read these rules aloud to their friends before play started. As children become familiar with a game they sometimes wanted to alter a rule. They were allowed to do this as long as the rules were agreed by everyone before play started. Often the new rules were better than the original. We felt that by taking a strong line over rules we were helping the children towards a better understanding of the need for the rules that we were imposing on them in real life.

Themes

We used a thematic approach when teaching, some themes lasting days while others were spread over a term. It was difficult at times to integrate mathematics into a theme as this approach does not always motivate all the mathematics needed, but we did make games which introduced concepts (particularly in the early stages) or gave practice in skills which were relevant to the stages of the children's mathematical development.

A favourite theme with very young children was nursery rhymes. Characters from the rhymes were sorted and matched and used as goals in counting on games. Other popular themes were Indians, cowboys, space, animals and the sea. By using the thematic approach certain concepts and skills could be introduced several times, giving more practice and lessening the chances of the children becoming bored. To integrate a board game used in this book into a particular theme, all you usually have to do is change the illustrations on the board and change the name.

Part 2

Games for the first three terms in school

When children first come to school we attempt to give them an innate understanding of number. Our mathematical games form part of a programme which provides the children with a rich diet of number experiences.

The games in this section show how we deal with mathematical relationships, matching activities and the understanding of early cardinal and ordinal numbers.

Contents

Setting Up Home

Aim

To give children practice with relationships.

Number of players 4

To make

Four boards, each 25cm x 31cm. Each board should show the interior of a room; a living room, a kitchen, a bathroom and a bedroom.

You will also need 20 smaller cards approximately 8cm x 5cm which show the furniture or household goods which the children will collect:

5 cards with a piece of living room furniture.

5 cards with kitchen furniture or kitchen sundries.

5 cards with bedroom furnishings.

5 cards with bathroom objects.

To play

Each child chooses a base board and then describes to the teacher the board and the reason for their choice. The teacher meanwhile shuffles the pack of small cards and puts them in a central position. The children then take turns in taking the top card, naming the object drawn on the card and placing it on their board if the item belongs to their room.

If the card does not belong, then a new pile of cards is started next to the original pack. The game is finished when one child has five objects on his board.

Note Some teachers may like to finish the game completely, waiting until all four players have five cards on their room base board.

the bathroom
the living room
the bedroom
the kitchen

Teddy's Patchwork Quilt

Aim

To give practice in matching colour and pattern.

Number of players 2

To make

Two base boards each 31cm x 40cm, as illustrated. A pack of cards approximately 8cm x 5cm covered with pieces of material which replicate the patches on the base board. Children like to see teddies in bed, but baby dolls, animals or people may be used instead.

To play

Each child chooses their base board. The pile of patches is placed between the players face downwards. Children take turns in removing a patch from the top of the pile. If the patch does not match one on the base board then a new pile of patches is started near to the original pack. The first child who covers all the patches on their quilt wins. Most children wait until both boards are filled before the game is seen as being finished.

Variation

This game may be made using materials of one colour but of different textures.

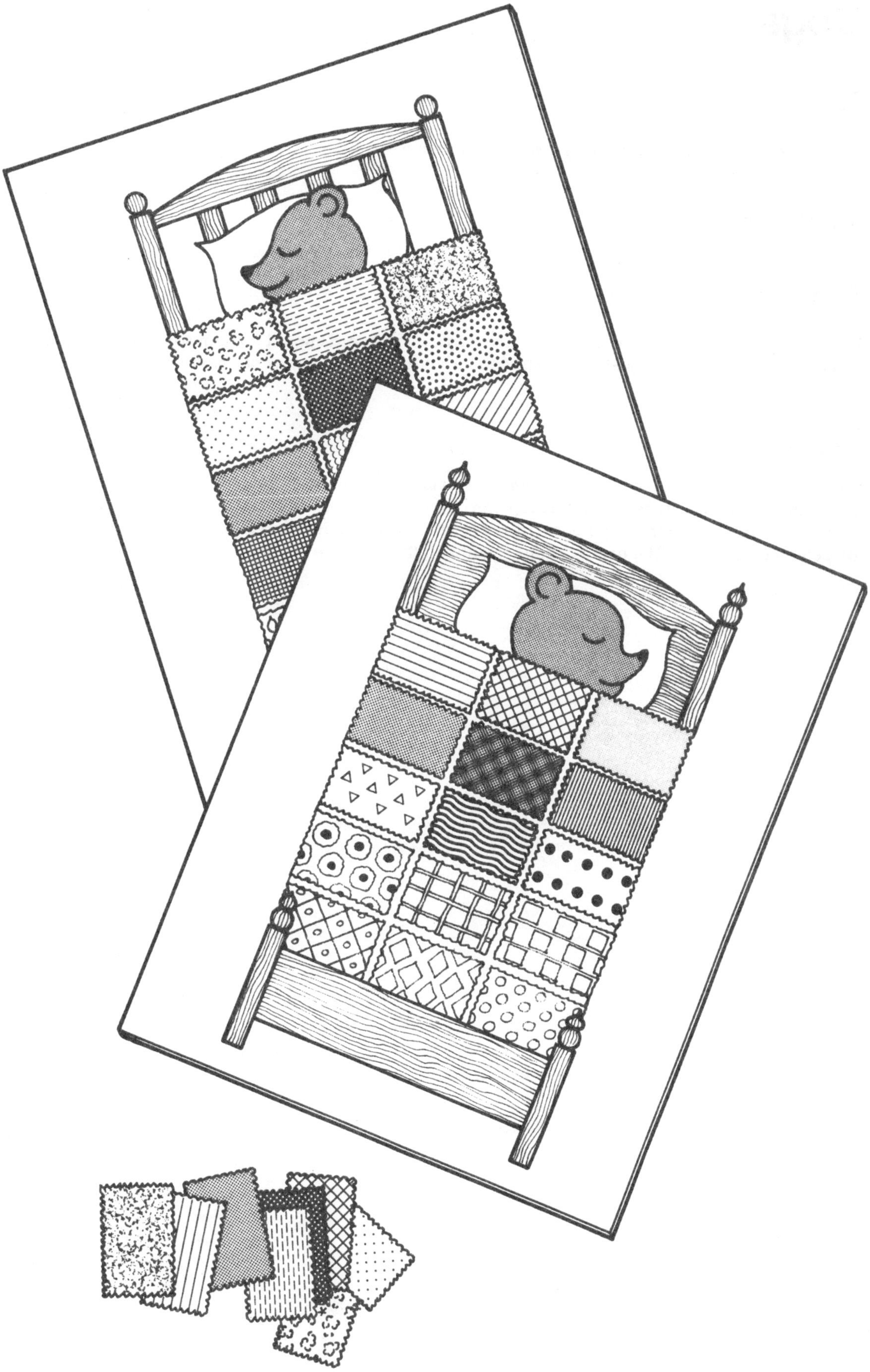

Dogs

Aim

To give practice in matching and visual discrimination.

Number of players 2

To make

Two base boards 41cm x 26cm each with five dogs. Each board should contain some dogs with hats and others without. The dogs should be traced individually on to a pack of smaller cards (13cm x 6cm).

To play

Each player chooses a base board and the pack of small dog cards is placed between players. Children then take turns removing the top card from the pack and attempt to match it with a dog on the base board. Should the dog not correspond with one on their board then the card is returned to the bottom of the pack. The game continues until all the dogs are covered.

Bees to the Beehive

Aim

To give practice in one-to-one matching and movement from left to right.

Number of players 2

To make

Two base boards, each 14cm x 51cm as illustrated. Each board has a flower, then five separate green rectangles and a beehive. (The flowers can be cut from seed merchants catalogues.)

The green rectangles are each 4cm x 6cm. The beehive may be traced. Twelve bee cards should be made and four blank cards.

To play

The pack of bee cards and blanks is shuffled and then placed between the players base boards. Children take turns removing the top card from the pack and they match bees to spaces, starting from the flower. When a blank card is removed from the pile then a turn is missed. The game continues until the line of bees reaches the beehive. This game introduces movement to the matching boards.

While the children are playing the teacher may like to ask questions such as, 'How many bees do you have?' 'Who has fewer (bees)?' 'Who has more?' 'How many more?'

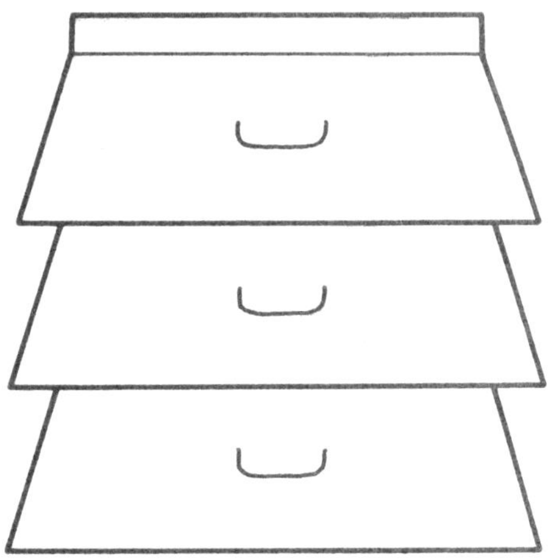

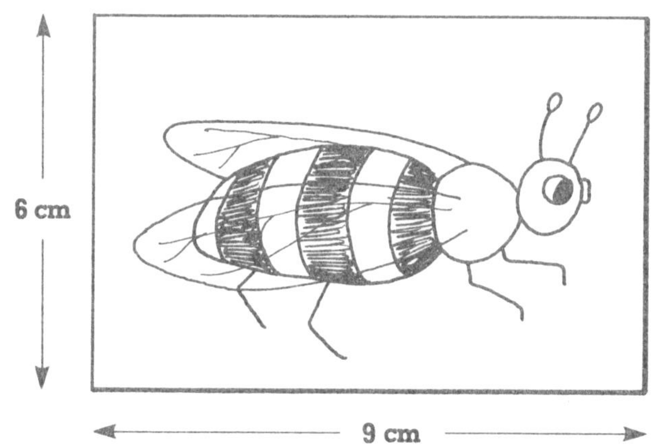

Teddy

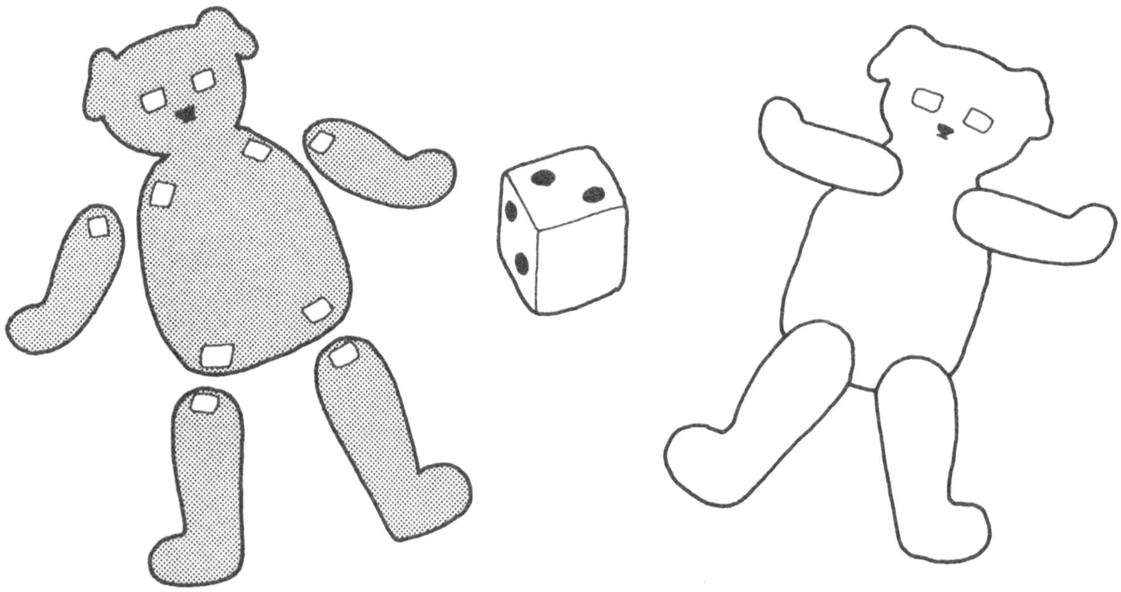

Aim

To give practice in the recognition of cardinal number 2 and understanding of the twoness of two.

Number of players 2

To make

Two teddy bodies as shown. The outline of the body may be traced on to cardboard, then covered with either felt or fur fabric. The two teddies should each be made of a different colour. Pairs of arms and legs are made in a similar fashion. Buttons can be used for the eyes.

A dice with four faces each with two dots and two blank faces is also required.

To play

Children choose bodies and sort out their arms, legs and eyes. They then take turns in throwing the dice. If they throw two dots, they can either place two legs, two arms or two eyes on the teddy body. Further throws are needed before the other limbs and eyes can be placed on the body. If a player throws a blank then a turn is missed.

This is the first game that has used a dice and although it is a very simple game very young children enjoy creating their own teddies in this way. The twoness of two is emphasised by the children matching the two dots on the dice with the two limbs or eyes.

Variation

Teddies can be made using two layers of felt which sandwich a thin layer of foam. The felt may be stitched around on a sewing machine. Velcro may be used to fasten on the eyes and the limbs.

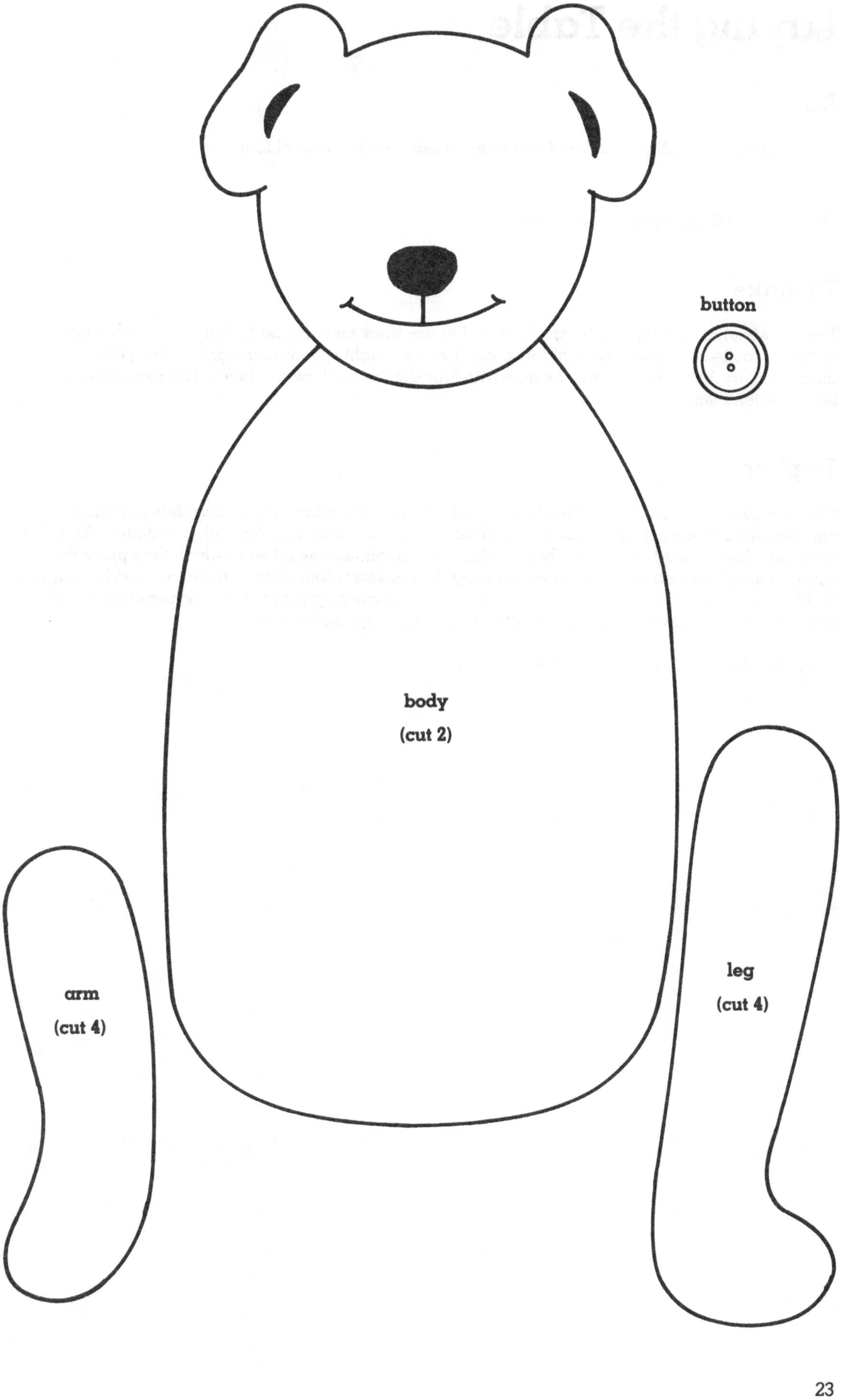
button
body
(cut 2)
arm
(cut 4)
leg
(cut 4)

Laying the Table

Aim

To recognise the cardinal number 4 and to emphasise the fourness of four.

Number of players 2 or more

To make

Two tableboards each 52cm x 65cm. Four doilies are stuck on each card. Eight dolls or teddies should be collected as well as eight forks, eight knives, eight spoons and eight plates. (We used plastic cutlery.) You will also need a dice with four dots on each of four faces. The remaining two faces are left blank.

To play

Children choose a base board, then take turns in throwing the dice. When four dots are thrown, children should seat dolls or teddies around the board, matching one doll with one doiley. After the dolls have been seated around the board, children can choose the order in which they place the cutlery and plates on their board after throwing the necessary four dots on the dice. Besides helping children with an awareness of the fourness of four this game brings out other mathematical facets. For example, the players will learn about left and right, top and bottom.

They will also learn how to lay a table correctly.

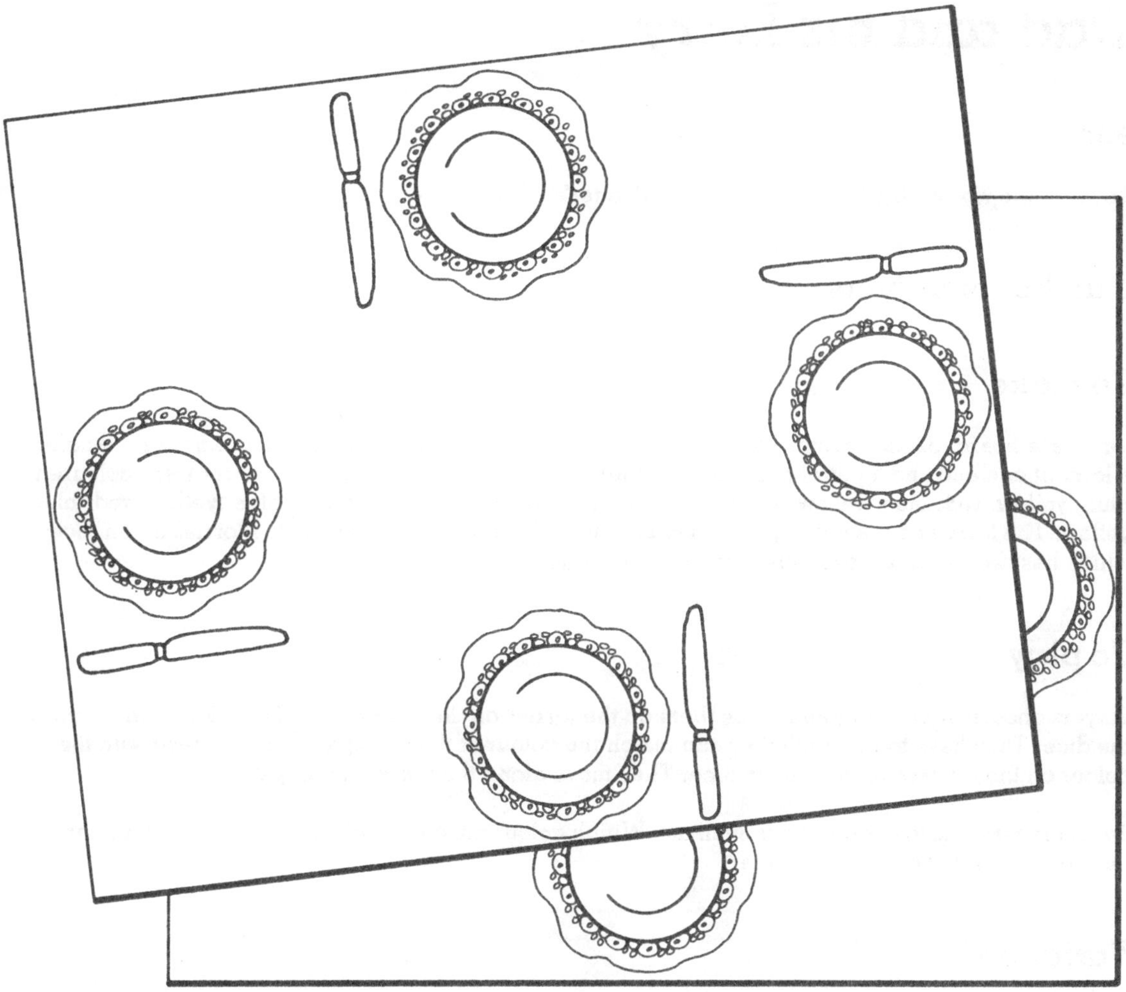

Dad and his Lorry

Aim

To learn the words, 'first', 'second', 'next' and 'after'.

Number of players 2

To make

One base board, 32cm x 51cm. There are two tracks on the board, each track having six rectangles, a lorry at one end and a petrol pump at the other end. The rectangles on the first track are coloured blue, yellow, red, blue, yellow, red and the second track rectangles are red, blue, yellow, red, blue, yellow. The lorry and the petrol pump may be traced. You will also need two toy lorries and a dice which has two red faces, two blue faces and two yellow faces.

To play

Players choose their lorries and place them on the lorries on the base board. They take turns to throw the dice. They have to wait until they can match the colour of the first space on the board with the colour on the top face of the thrown dice. They move along the board in this way.

Teachers may like to ask questions such as, 'Which colour must you get next?' 'Which colour came before red?' 'What comes after blue?'

Variation

This game may be made with soldiers racing to get to the fort.

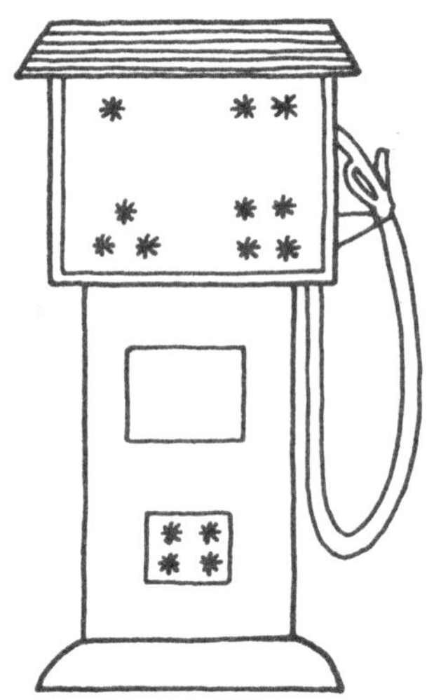

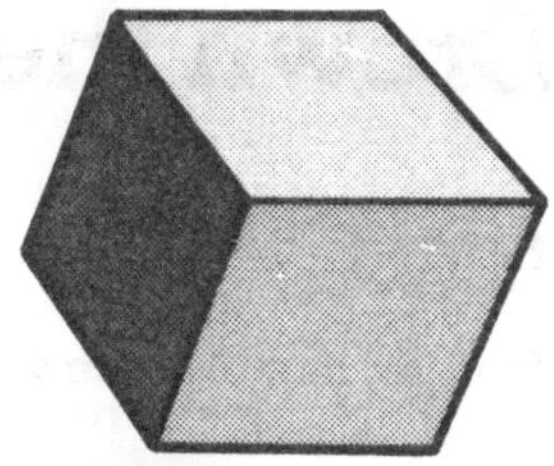

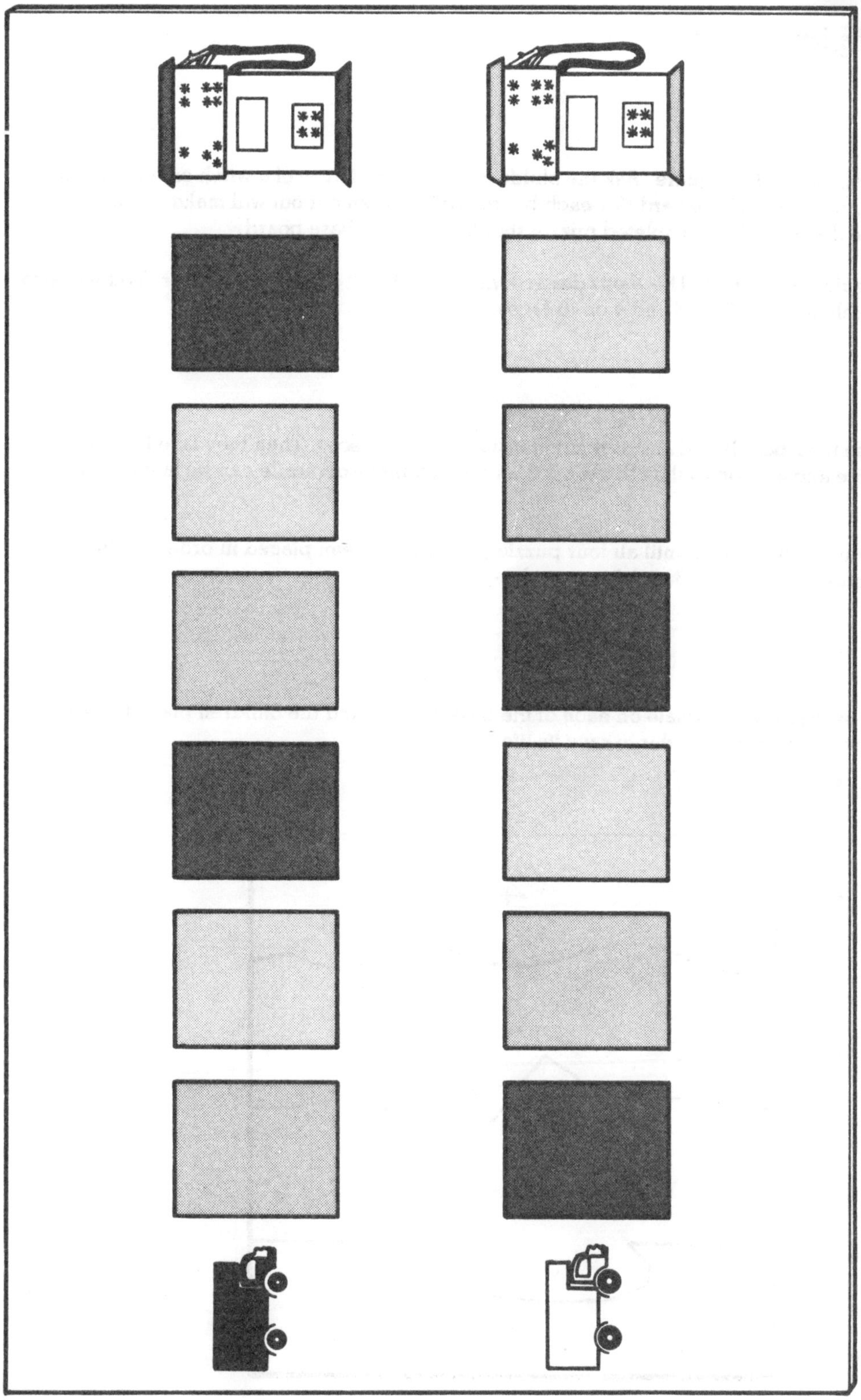

Drown the Witch

Aim

To order numbers 1 to 4.

Number of players 2

To make

Two base boards, each 28cm square. Ask the children to paint a picture of a witch on each of the base boards. Four pieces of blue card (for each board) which when cut out will make a jigsaw puzzle, as in the diagram. The completed puzzle should cover the base board.

The puzzles should be different. These puzzles are water which will drown the witches. You will also need a dice which has 1, 1, 2, 2, 3 and 4 on its faces.

To play

Children choose their base board and sort out their four puzzle pieces. Then they take turns in throwing the dice and as soon as they throw a 1 then the first piece of puzzle can be laid on the witch.

Children continue to throw dice until all four puzzle pieces have been placed in order on the witches. They must throw a 1, 2, 3 and 4 to complete the puzzle.

Variation

This game can be made with a whale on each of the base boards, and the children place the water puzzle pieces over the whale in order to save its life.

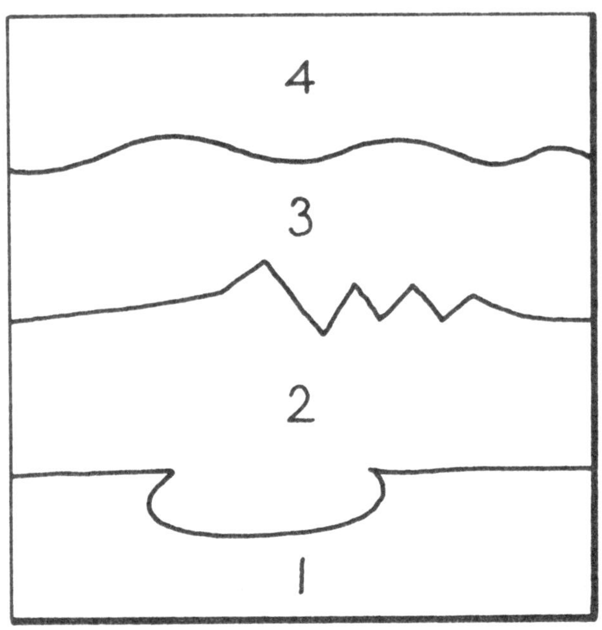

1
3
4
3
2

Number Rummy

Aim

To give children practice in ordering sets of numbers between 1 and 6.

Number of players 2

To make

56 cards, each approximately 10cm x 14cm:

6 cards should show an empty set.

6 cards should show a set with 1 object.

6 cards should show a set of 2 objects.

6 cards should show a set of 3 objects.

6 cards should show a set of 4 objects.

6 cards should show a set of 5 objects.

6 cards should show a set of 6 objects.

(We made our cards using picture labels but stamps can be used.)

To play

Players place the pack of cards upside down between them on the table, and take turns in removing the top card from the pile. They try to make a run or a set as illustrated opposite. Unwanted cards should be placed face upwards at the side of the original pack. Opponents may take from this pile if the top card is one which will help create a run or a set. The winner is the player who makes most runs or sets.

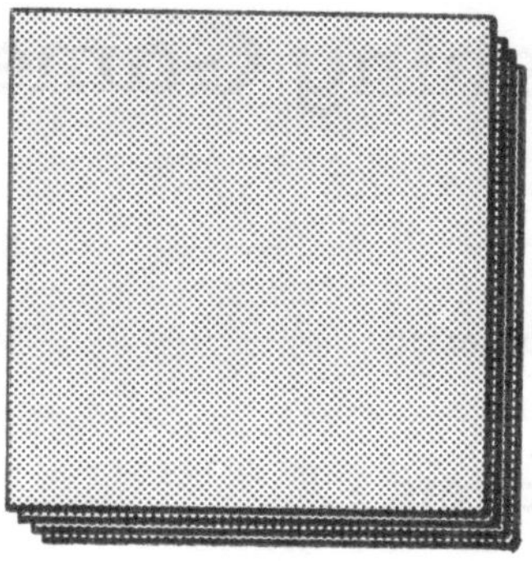

a run

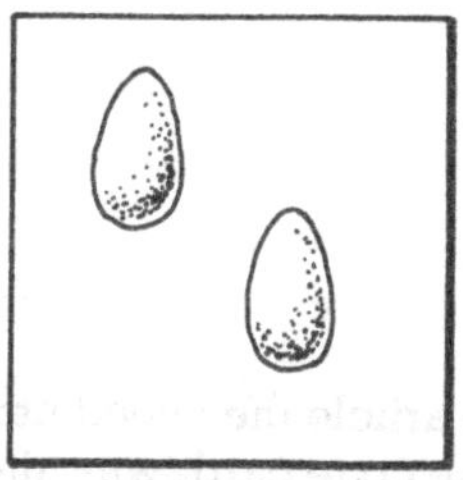  

a set

The Washing Game

Aim

To give practice in ordering.

Number of players 2

To make

Two boards 47cm x 32cm as illustrated. Also two pairs of blue jeans cut from card, two red shirts, two pairs of green pants, two yellow jumpers and two brown socks.

Five code cards each 10cm x 12cm.

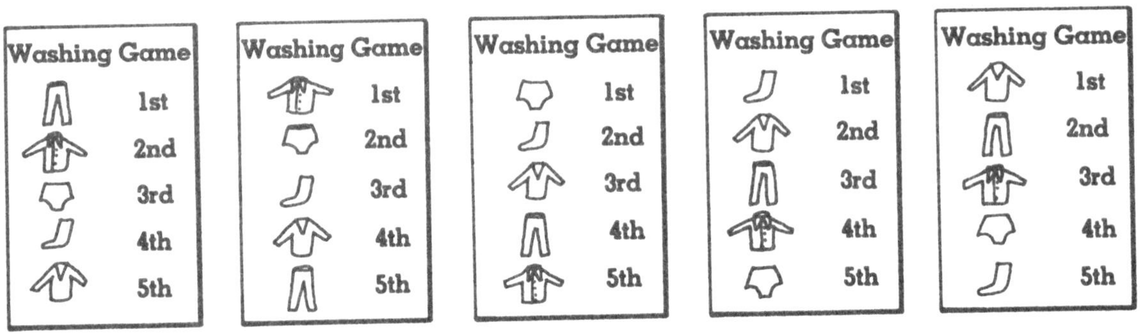

The dice should have a different item of clothing on each face using the blue jeans, pair of green pants, yellow jumper, red shirt, a brown sock and a washing basket.

To play

Each player chooses a base board. The code cards are shuffled and placed face down in between the two players. The card on top of the pack is turned over. This card decides the order that the washing is to be hung on the line. Players then take turns in throwing the dice. They have to wait until they have thrown on the dice the article at the top of the list before they can put it on the line on the left hand side, under the first two pegs.

e.g.

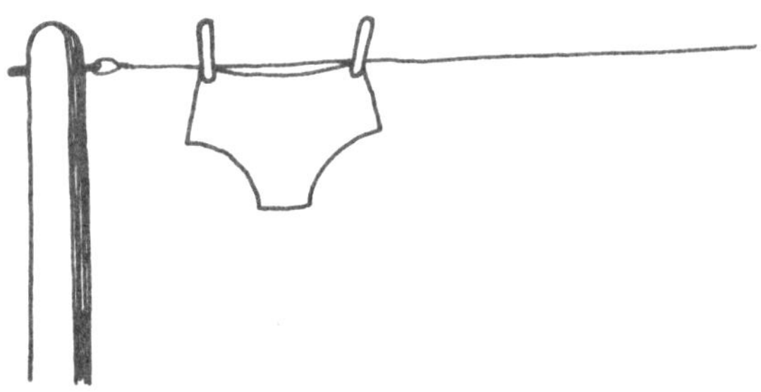

If a player throws the washing basket then they can place on the line the article they need next. The first player to hang five articles on the line in the order determined by the code card, wins the game.

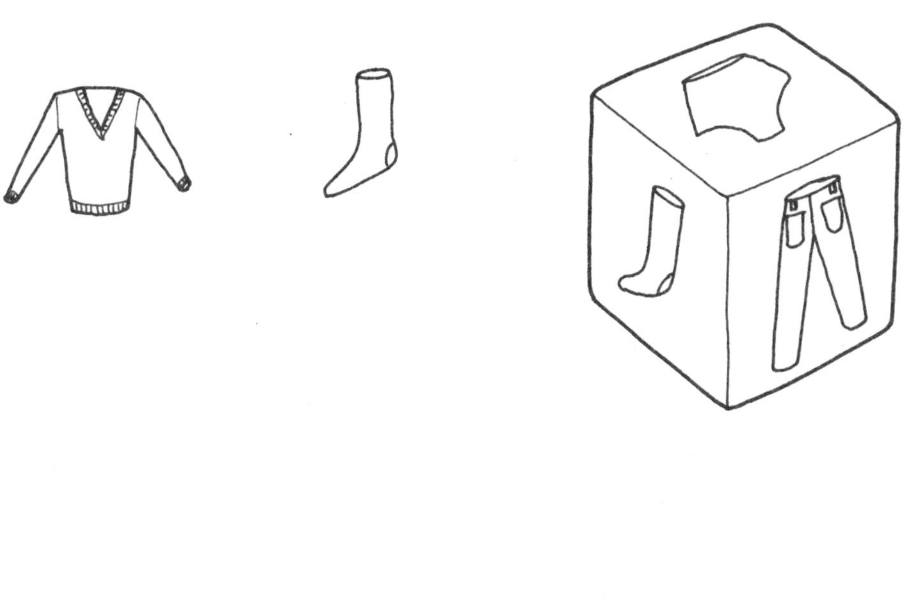

Counting on games

We found that when our children had had experience with early number and were ready for number line activities they could not count on correctly. We made large stepping stones in the playground and on the classroom floor and used our display boards to make large pictures with the children. A popular one was a row of houses with numbered doors and then a postman was made and the children were able to move him along to deliver letters. Instructions such as, 'Deliver a letter to house number 3, now move on two houses, what number are you at?' were enjoyed by the children and made us realise that there were a lot of games that could be made to practise this concept.

The first games in this section have movements from one space to the next using a counter smaller than a space. The children soon learn to move on correctly as it increases the chance of winning!

Home made dice with two ones, two twos and two threes are best at this stage because the children will not get 'lost' with large numbers in their counting on. Commercially produced dice can be used later to develop the concept when children have become competent.

Contents

Ducks to the Pond

Aim

To give practice in counting on using large separate spaces.

Number of players 2

To make

One base board 32cm x 51cm. At the left hand side of the base board are two ducks and at the right hand side an attractive-looking pond. There are ten stepping stones between the ducks and the pond. The ducks may be traced.

You will also need two ducks for counters and a dice marked with two ones, two twos and two threes.

To play

Players take turns to throw the dice and move the appropriate number of places. The game continues until a player reaches the pond.

Variation

Many games using this same principal can be made, e.g. dogs going to their kennels, Indians to their teepee, etc.

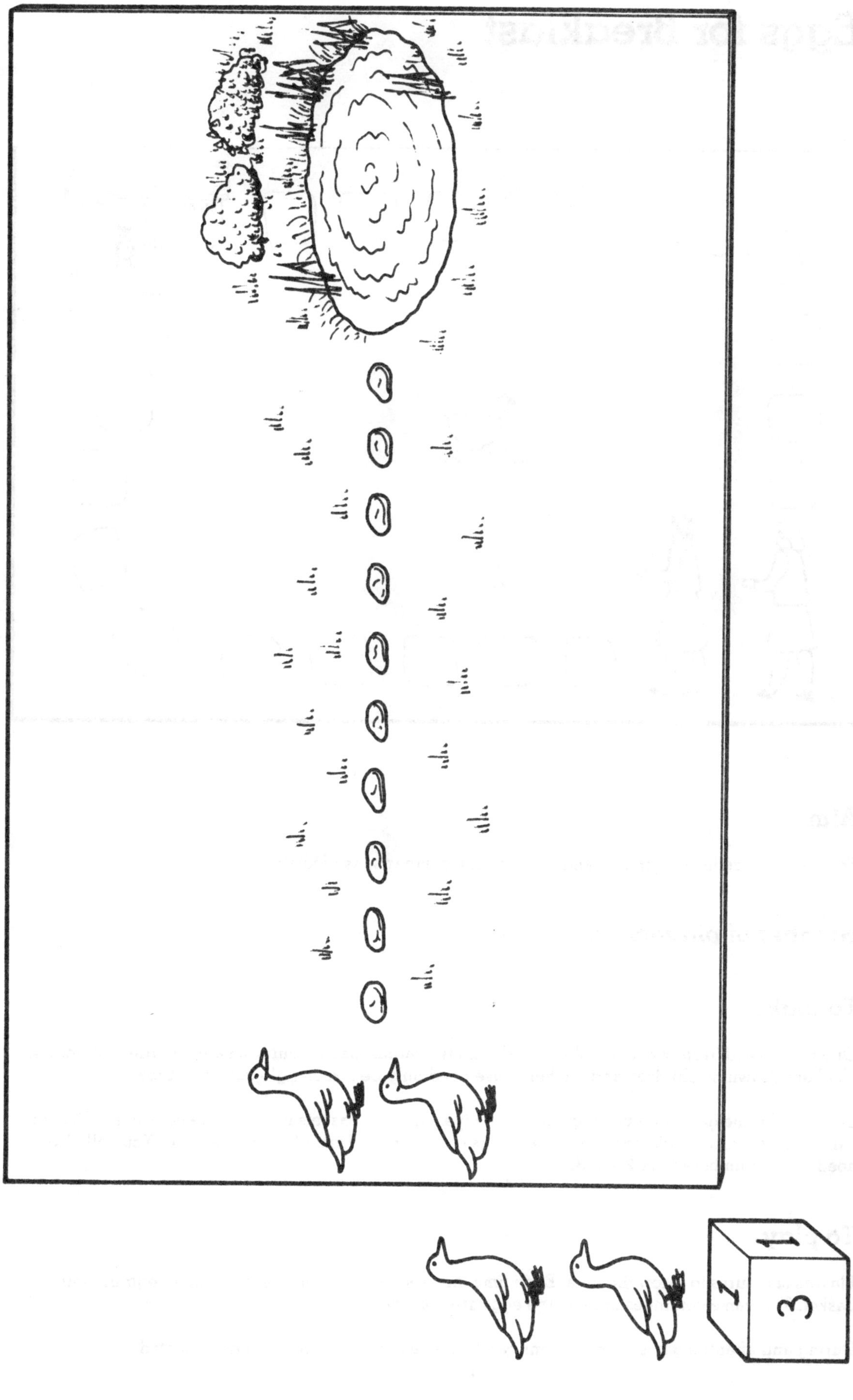

Eggs for Breakfast

Aim

To give practice in counting on and to introduce comparisons of totals.

Number of players 2

To make

One base board 51cm x 63cm as illustrated. The two ladies may be cut from a mail order catalogue, chickens drawn by children and the henhouse need only be a rectangle coloured brown.

Counters for the game can be model farmers wives, the two baskets in which the eggs are collected can be made from matchboxes and seven eggs can be made from clay or plasticine. You will also need a dice numbered 1,1,2,2,3,3.

To play

Players take turns to throw the dice. Each time they reach the henhouse they put an egg in their basket. The game continues until all the eggs are collected.

During and after the game, comparisons can be made of the number of eggs collected.

Rapunzel

Aim

To give practice in counting on.

Number of players 2

To make

One base board 31.5cm x 51cm as illustrated. Old fairy tale books produce useful pictures to cut out and stick on the game boards. You also need two counters and a dice numbered 1-6.

To play

Players decide who is the witch and who is the prince and place their counters on the respective pictures. They take turns throwing the dice and move up Rapunzel's hair according to the number thrown on the dice. If the witch or the prince land on the same place, they push each other down the tower.

The game continues until one player reaches Rapunzel.

This is the first time that a hazard has been introduced.

A Visit to the Zoo

Aim

To give practice in counting on.

Number of players 2

To make

One base board, 63.5cm x 51cm, as illustrated. The animals in the zoo can be traced from the animals drawn here or cut from gift wrapping paper. The five animals should also be traced on to pink and blue card and cut in rectangles. You will also need two counters and a dice numbered 1-6.

To play

One player takes the pile of pink animal cards and gives the pile of blue cards to his opponent. Each player then turns up his top card to determine which animal is visited first. The players take turns to throw the dice and move the counter accordingly towards the animal shown on top of the pile. On reaching the animal at one of the viewing points, the animal card is left as proof of having visited that part of the zoo. The next card in the pile is then turned over and the player moves his counter to visit the next animal according to the numbers thrown on the dice. The game continues until the players have visited all the animals in the zoo.

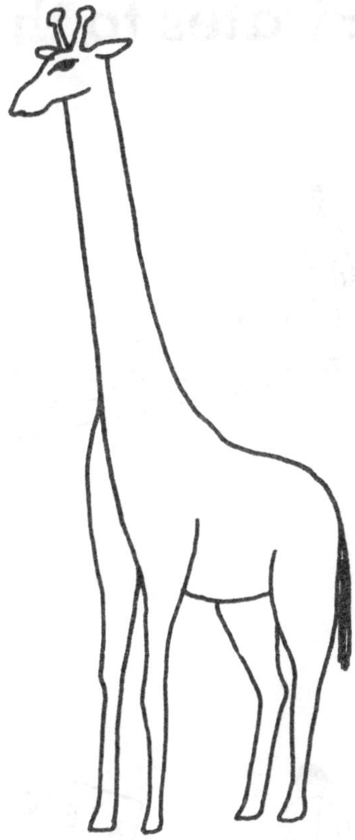

Pirates to the Ship

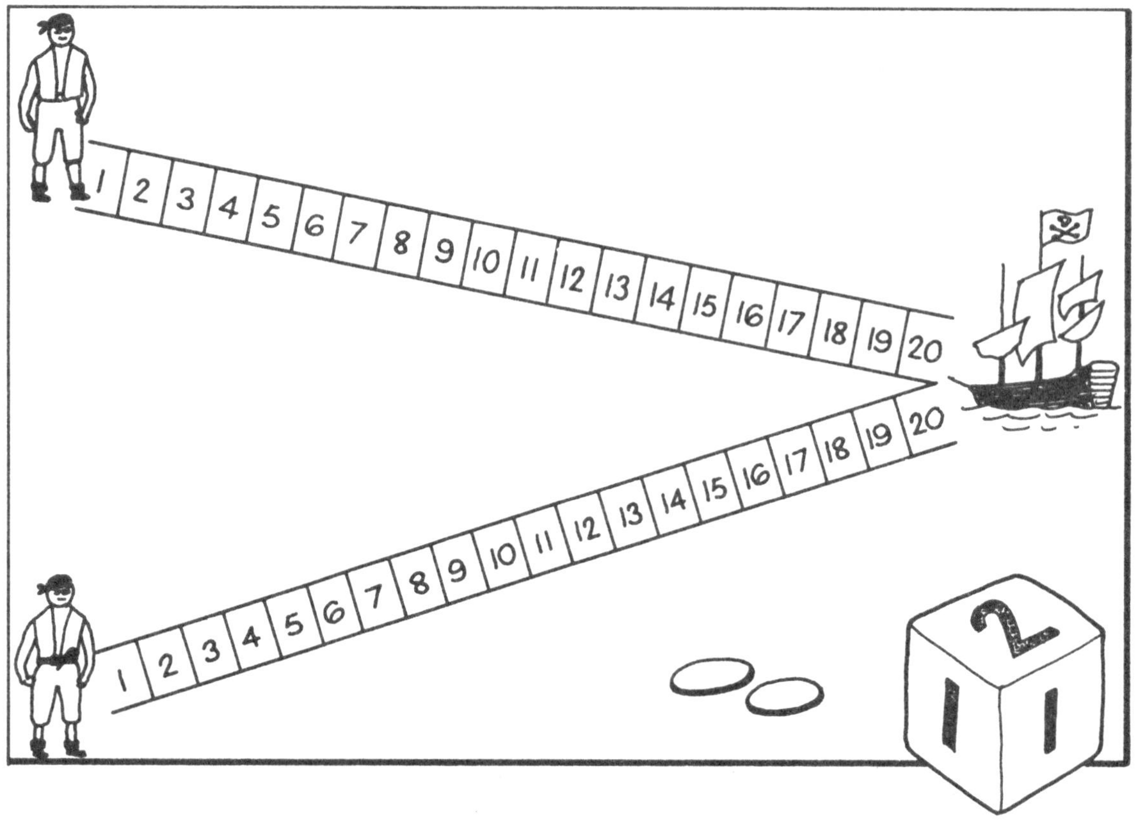

Aim

To give practice in counting on.

Number of players 2

To make

One base board 47cm x 32cm as illustrated, a dice numbered 1, 2, 3, 4, 1 and 2 and two counters.

To play

The players choose a counter and place it on a pirate. Both players throw the dice and the one with the lowest score begins. They move along the board according to the number thrown on the dice. The first player to reach the ship sails away.

This is the first time that numbers have been written on the track and children can be made aware that if they start on 2 and throw a 3, then the counter will move to 5, etc.

On the Farm

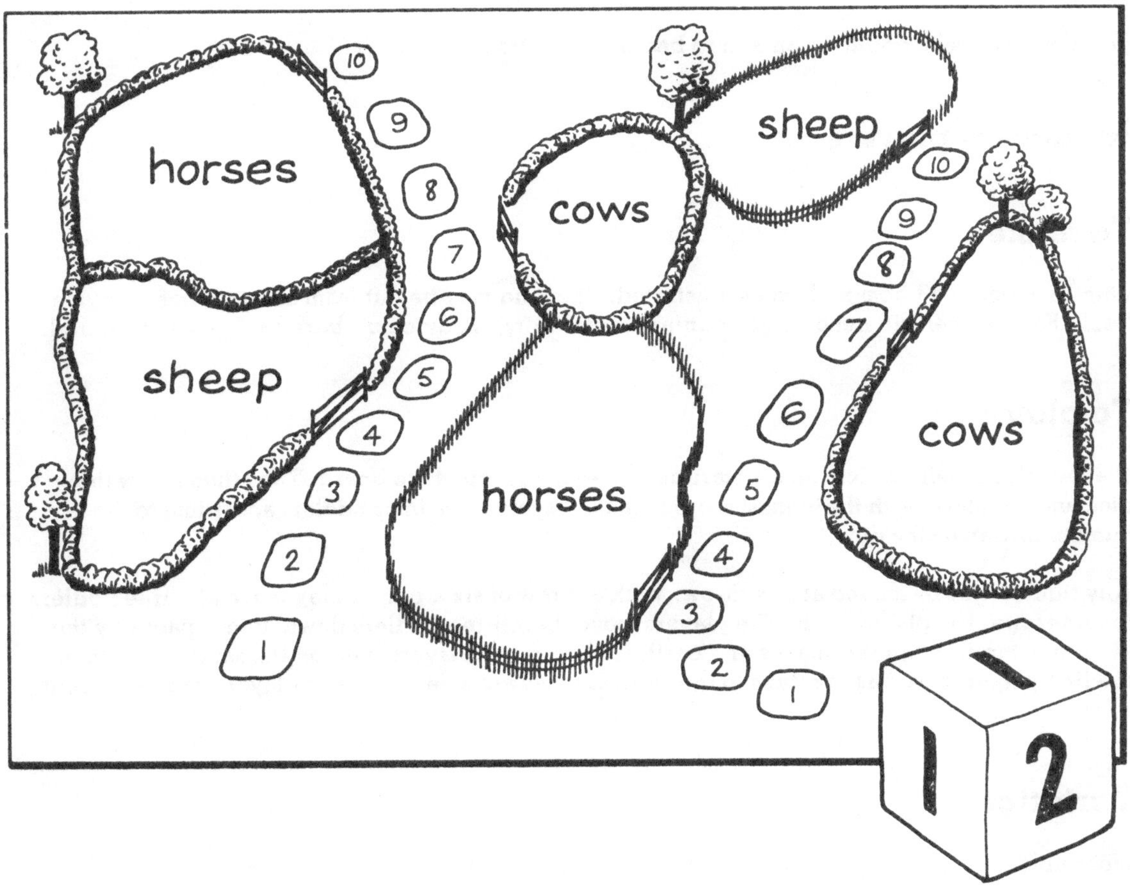

Aim

To give practice in sorting and counting on.

Number of players 2

To make

One base board 51cm x 63.5cm as illustrated, two counters (farmers), eight or more of three toy farm animals and a dice marked 1, 1, 2, 2, 3, 3.

To play

Players choose their farmer counters and place them in their starting places. They then take turns throwing the dice and move on the appropriate number of spaces. When a player reaches a gate, he sorts an appropriate animal into the field. Play continues until all the animals have been sorted into the correct fields.

Children can then discuss who has most sheep or fewest cows.

Old King Cole

Aim

To give practice in counting on and to begin to use strategies.

Number of players 2

To make

One base board 63.5cm x 51cm as illustrated. The king may be cut from an old nursery rhyme book. Each player will need three counters (or fiddlers). A dice numbered 1-6 is also required.

To play

Players place their fiddlers on the starting places at the top of the board. They then throw the dice and the player with the highest score begins. Players move their fiddlers according to the number thrown on the dice.

Any fiddler may be moved at any throw. With a throw of six a player may move all three fiddlers together, i.e. two places each. The players move their three fiddlers down to the spaces by the king, moving through the spaces and castles. Should two players land on the same space then the first player there has to return to the start. Castles are safe areas and players cannot be sent back.

Variation

More able players could use two dice thus involving a variety of number work.

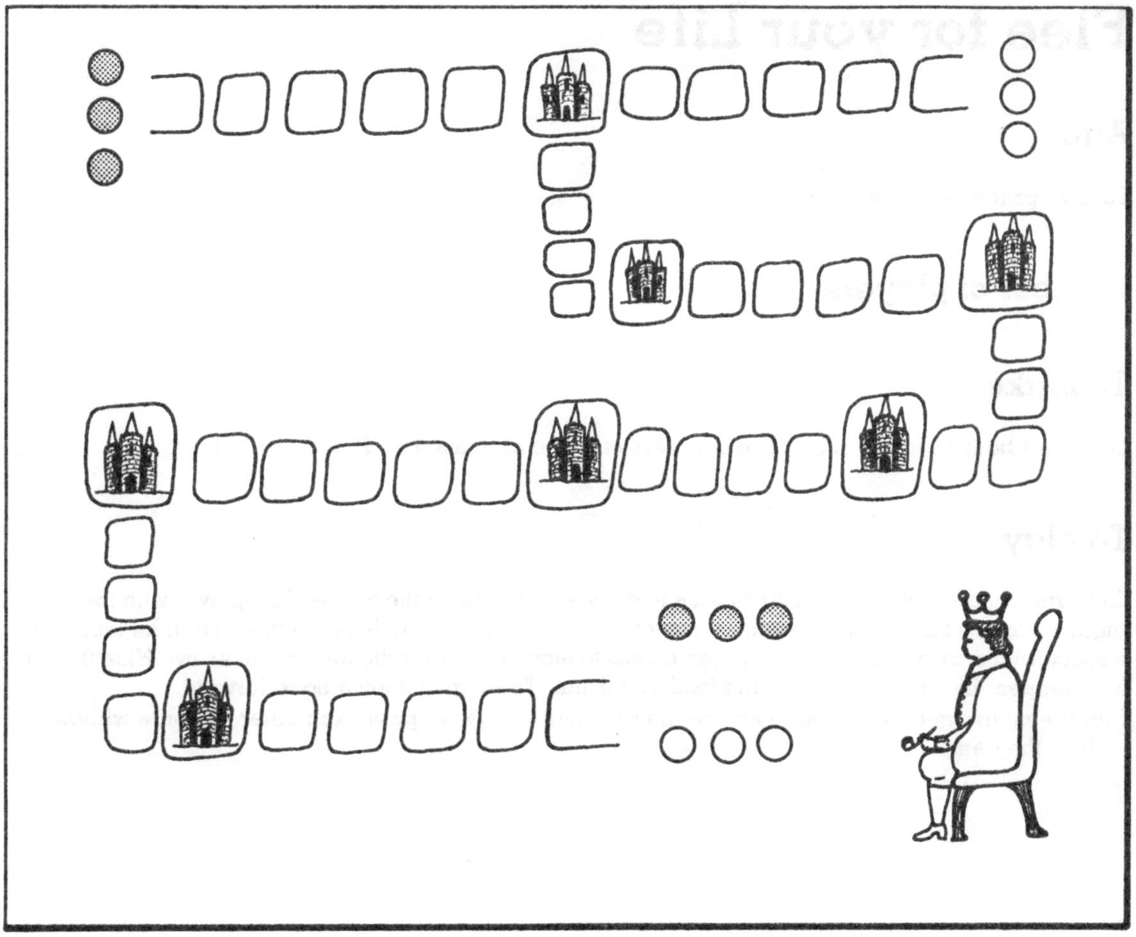

Flee for your Life

Aim

To give practice in counting on.

Number of players 2

To make

One base board 47cm x 32cm, two counters and one dice marked 1, 2, 3, 1, 2, 3.

To play

Children choose counters and throw dice to decide who is to be the mouse. The player with the highest score is the mouse. The mouse moves first according to the throw on the dice. If he lands on a space with a hazard and an arrow then he has to move back as indicated by the arrow. Nice things also happen, like the animals finding food and drink. These give them a boost forward.
Can the mouse get into the hole before the cat? (Animals may pass each other en route without ending the game.)

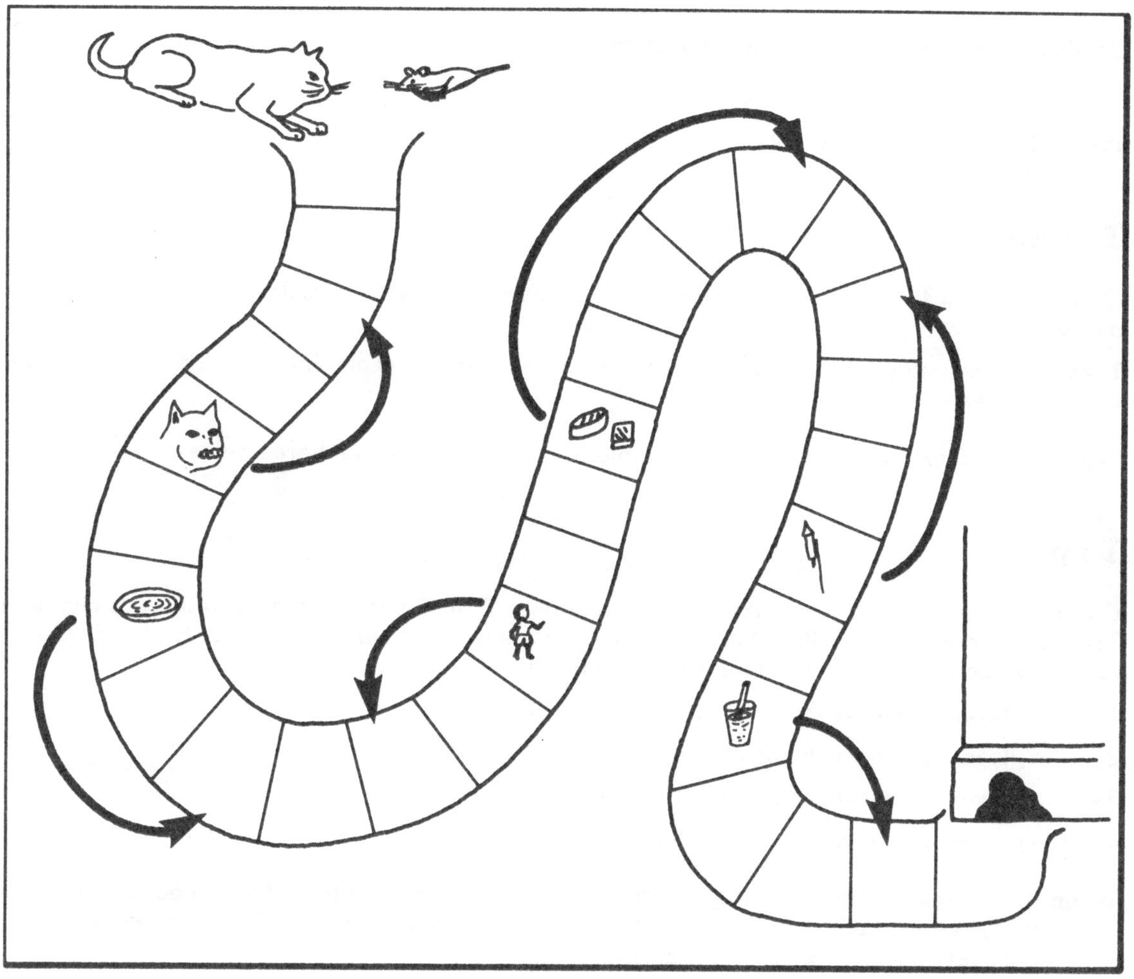

2
1
1

Noah's Ark

Aim

To give practice in counting on and partitioning numbers.

Number of players 2

To make

One base board 47cm x 32cm as illustrated, four counters (Noah's animals) for each player, made as follows:

Take four red Unifix cubes and into the top holes insert drawings of a lion, an elephant, a giraffe and a monkey.

Repeat these four counters using another coloured cube. A dice numbered 1-6 is also needed.

To play

Children throw the dice to determine the start of play. The player with the highest score begins. The players now try to get their four animals to the ark first as Noah has room for four and will only take a set. Players move according to the throw on the dice:

1 — the player may move the elephant one space

2 — the player may move the lion two spaces

3 — the player may move the giraffe three spaces

4 — the player may move the monkey four spaces.

When a 5 is thrown on the dice, the player may move his elephant forward five spaces, or his lion four spaces and his elephant one space, or his giraffe three spaces and his lion two, etc. A throw of 6 may similarly be split amongst the animals.

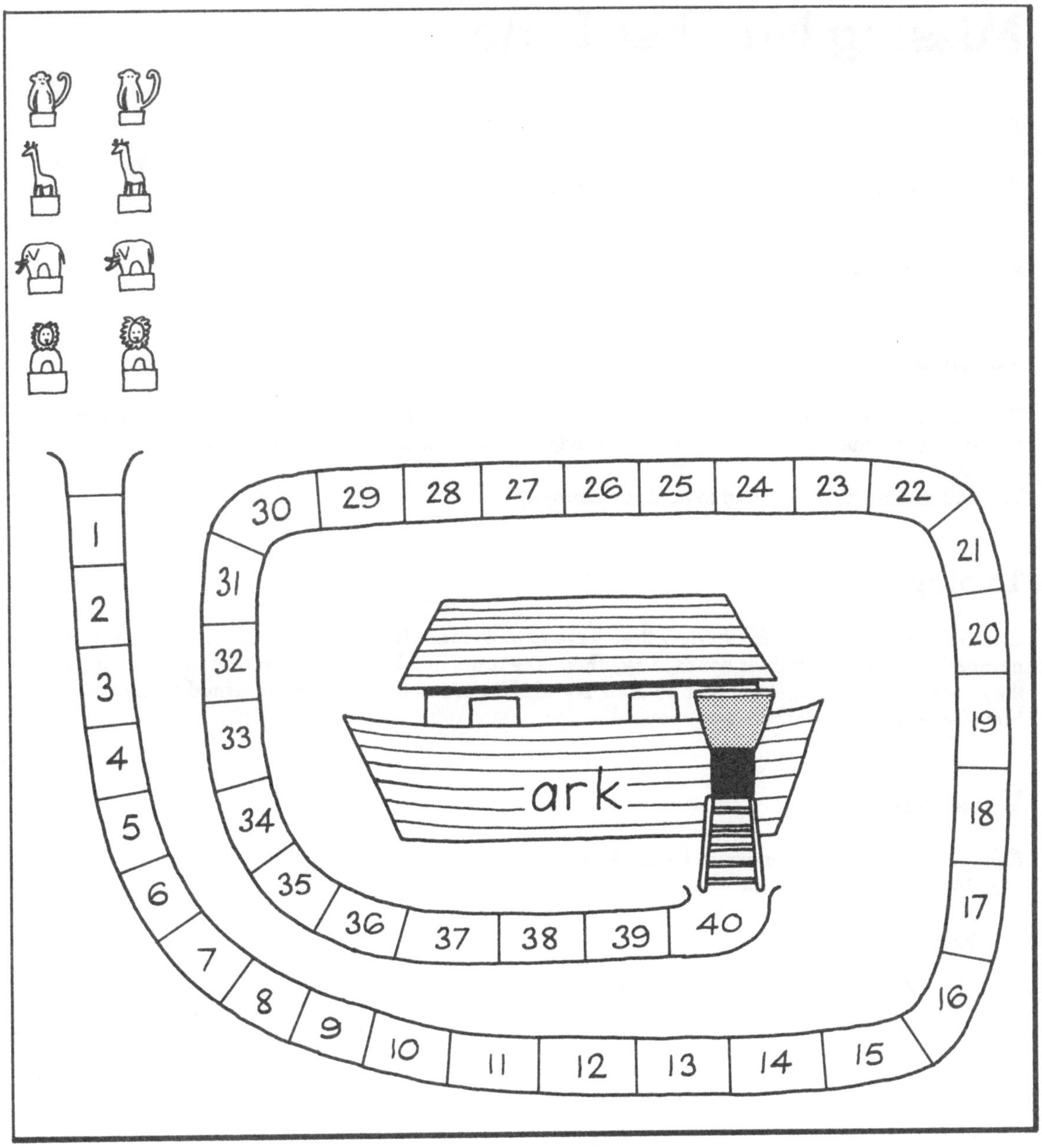
1
2
3
4
5
6
7
8
9
10
11
12
13
14
15
16
17
18
19
20
21
22
23
24
25
26
27
28
29
30
31
32
33
34
35
36
37
38
39
40
ark

2
1
3

Missing Number Lotto

Aim

To give practice in putting numbers in order through counting.

Number of players 2

To make

Two base boards as illustrated. Ten numbered counters which replace the numbers omitted from the board, e.g. on the top line, 5 and 7 are missed out, on the second line the 6 is omitted.

You will also need a small bag to hold the counters.

To play

Children choose a base board. They then have to look carefully and by counting, decide which numbers are left out on their board. They then take turns in taking a counter from the bag and see if they have a space for that number on their board. Discarded numbers are returned to the bag. The first player to cover all their spaces wins.

Variation

Runs of larger numbers may also be used:
e.g. 38 □ 40 □ 42 □ 44

59 □ 61 □ 63

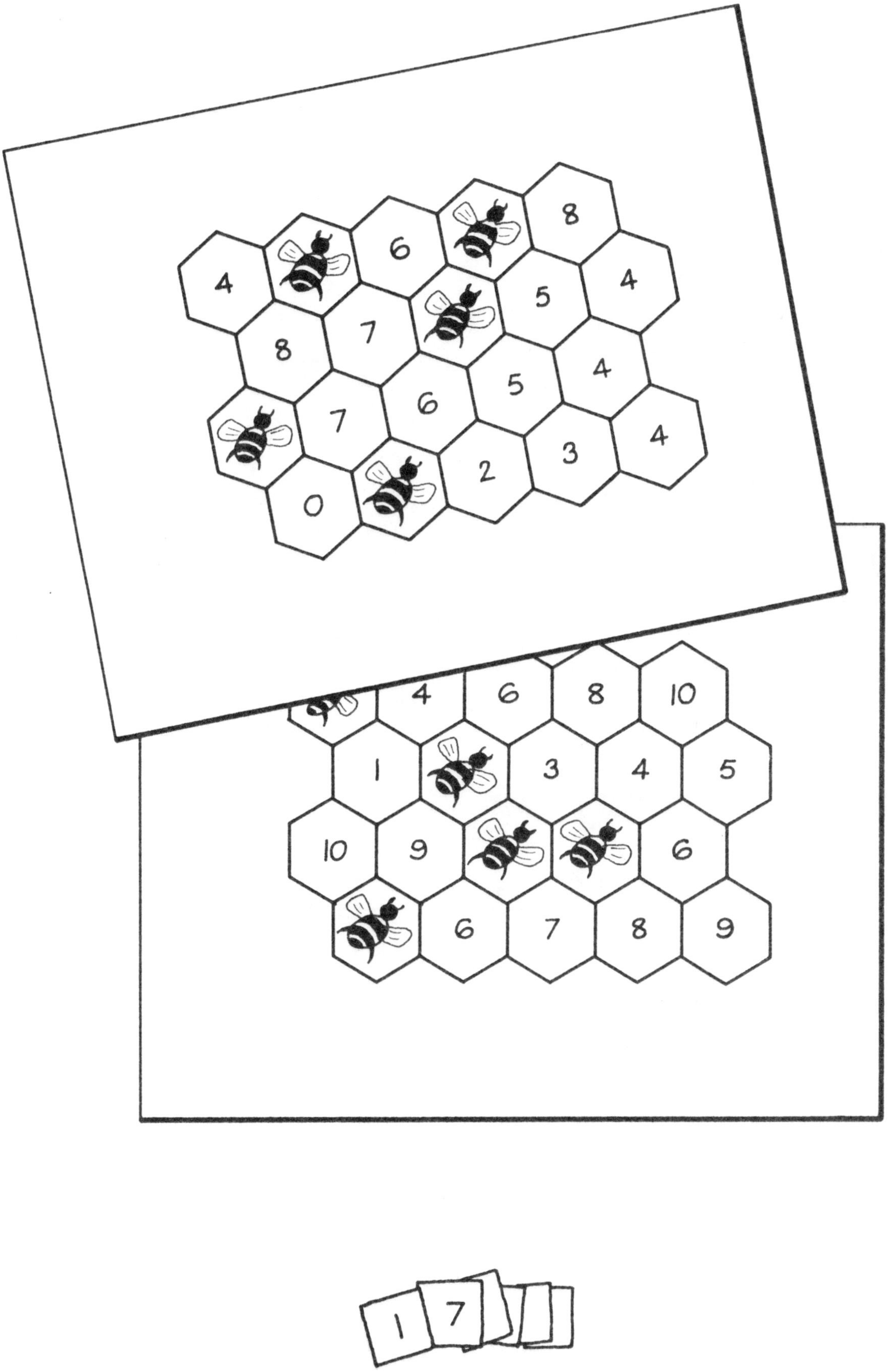
4
6
8
8
7
5
4
7
6
5
4
0
2
3
4
4
6
8
10
1
3
4
5
10
9
6
6
7
8
9
1
7

Games for addition, subtraction, multiplication and number facts

We are constantly looking for alternative ways of giving children practice in learning and using number facts; pages of sums are not the answer. We aim for instant recall. Games give children a reason for knowing facts, it helps them win! The games that follow provide various interesting and exciting ways in which these facts can be practised.

Contents

Sink the Ships

Aim

To give practice in addition.

Number of players 2

To make

Two base boards 31.5cm x 51cm as illustrated. There are five ships on each card. Ten sea cards should be cut from card. These cards should cover the ships and the edges can be cut as illustrated.

You also need playing cards:

0 + 10	6 + 4	6 + 3	4 + 5
1 + 9	7 + 3	3 + 6	1 + 8
2 + 8	8 + 2	7 + 2	8 + 1
3 + 7	9 + 1	2 + 7	4 + 3
4 + 6	10 + 0	5 + 4	3 + 4
5 + 5			

To play

Players choose their base board and take five sea pieces. They take turns in removing the top card from the pack of cards and doing the addition sum which is written on it. If the answer to the sum is 10 then the player sinks his opponent's ship by covering it with a sea card.

The game continues until one player has sunk all of his opponent's ships.

Variations

Subtraction and multiplication sums can be written on the cards.

Catch the Fly

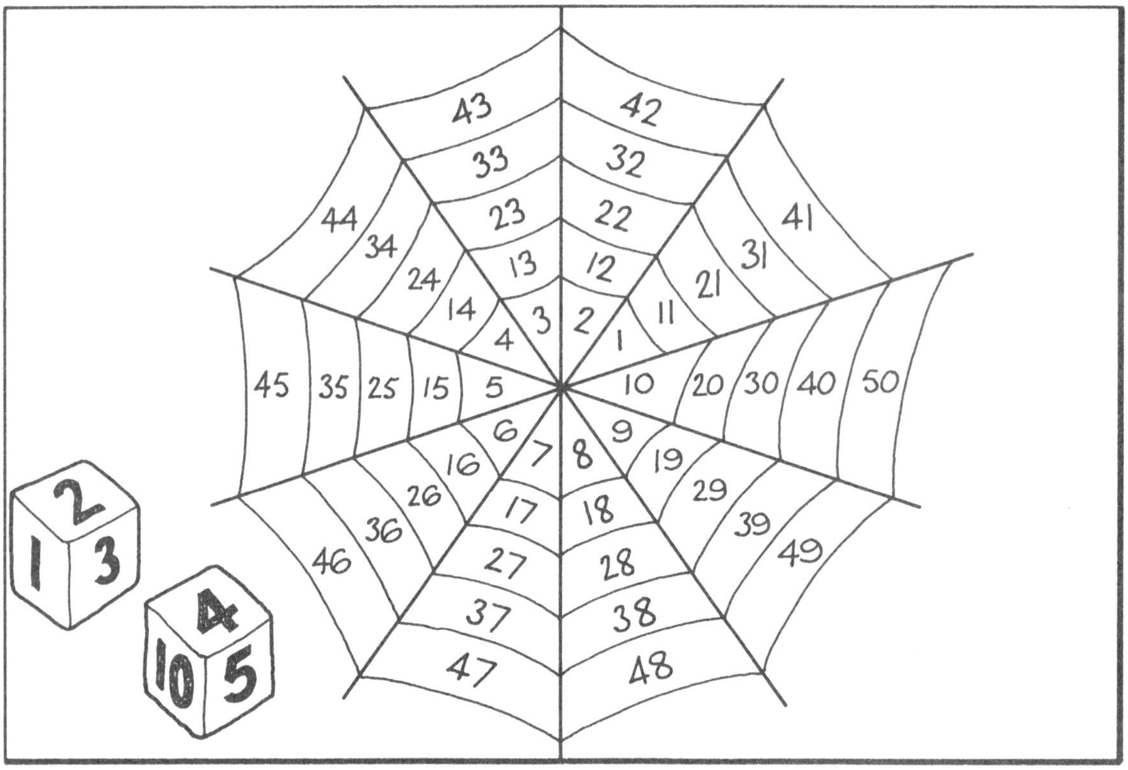

Aim

To give practice in adding on 5 and 10.

Number of players 2

To make

One base board 43.5cm x 51cm as illustrated, two counters and two dice. One dice for the spider numbered 1-6 and one for the fly numbered 10, 5, 5, 4, 3, 2.

To play

The fly throws his dice first and proceeds from the centre of the web, counting on through the spaces of the web according to the number shown on the thrown dice. The spider takes his turn and the game continues until either the fly escapes or the spider catches him.

After playing this game several times children will become aware of the pattern of adding 10.

The Hundred Game

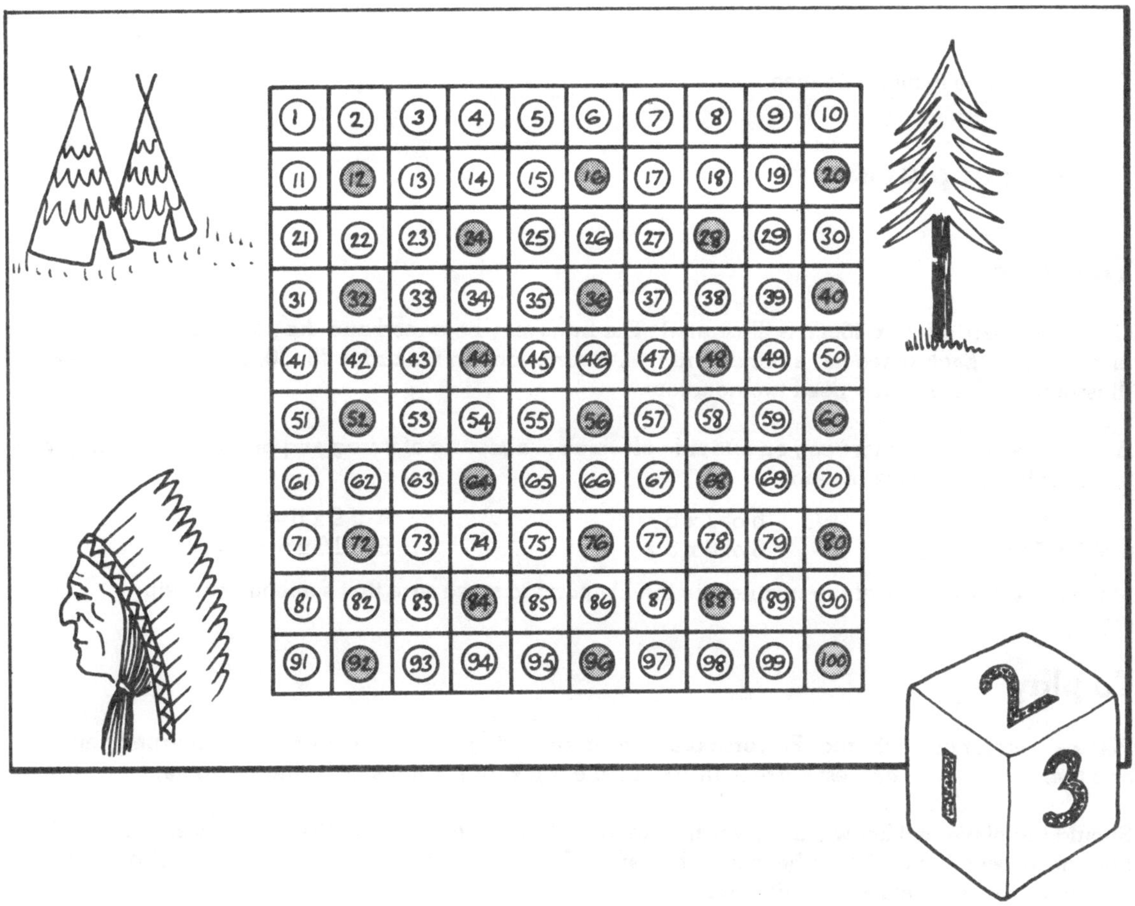

Aim

To give practice in adding and subtracting 10.

Number of players 2

To make

One base board, 32cm x 50cm as illustrated, two counters, and one dice numbered 1-6. The spots are self-adhesive coloured spots. The children may like to illustrate the board.

To play

Players take turns to throw the dice and move to the appropriate number by counting on. When a player lands on a green spot he moves on 10, and when he lands on a yellow spot he moves back 10.

As with the *Catch the Fly* game, this game helps the child learn what happens when 10 is added and also subtracted.

Note A variety of base boards can be made using other number patterns.

Jumping Frogs

Aim

To give practice in multiplication.

Number of players 2

To make

One base board 41cm x 46cm as illustrated. The frogs may be traced and the pond cut from an old picture book. Each space has a number in it with variations on the order 25, 30, 35, 40, 45, 50 (see illustration). You will also need two counters.

A frog master card 9cm x 6cm, on one side of which is a picture of a frog and on the reverse the five times table. Also a pack of cards:

6 of 5 x 5 =	6 of 7 x 5 =	6 of 9 x 5 =
6 of 6 x 5 =	6 of 8 x 5 =	6 of 10 x 5 =

Make three extra cards of the sum next to the lily pond to make sure that someone can win.

To play

Place a counter on each frog. Players take turns in removing the top card from the upturned pack and then move to the nearest correct answer on the track (this is not a counting on game).

Should the player not know the answer he can look at the reverse side of the frog master card, and find the answer. A turn has to be missed however. The frog master card can also be used to check an opponent's answer with no penalty involved.

Note Games can be made for all multiplication tables.

30
25
30
35
40
45
50
30
35
25
45
40
50
45
50
25
30
35
40
30
25
40
35
50
45
35
30
25
50
45
40
45
40
35
30
25
50
35
50
35
50
25
30
35
40
45
40
45
50
25
30
50

6x5

A Visit to the Castle

Aim

To give practice in addition with money.

Number of players 2 and a banker

To make

One base board 51cm x 63.5cm, as illustrated. Different coloured cars can be cut from old books or gift wrapping paper. A picture of a local castle can be pasted on the board. The gummed money stuck on the tracks must add to the same totals down each side of the track.

You will also need two cards for counters, some money and a dice numbered 1, 2, 5, 10, 20, 10.

To play

Players place their counters on the car of their choice and throw the dice, the highest number begins. They collect money to pay for their petrol by throwing the dice and collecting the amount shown from the banker.

The player then has to decide how many spaces he can move through according to the amount of money he has accumulated. If he has 40p from the banker then he may move through as many spaces as it takes to use up that money, or he may choose to hold his money and make fewer but more dramatic moves. When the track splits one player should go one way and the other player in the opposite direction. All the time children are constantly adding the newly thrown amount to what they already have or are doing subtraction sums such as, 'I have 5p in my hand. It costs 4p to move into that next space. How much will I have left? Will it be enough to take me into the next space?' The winner is the first player to get inside the castle.

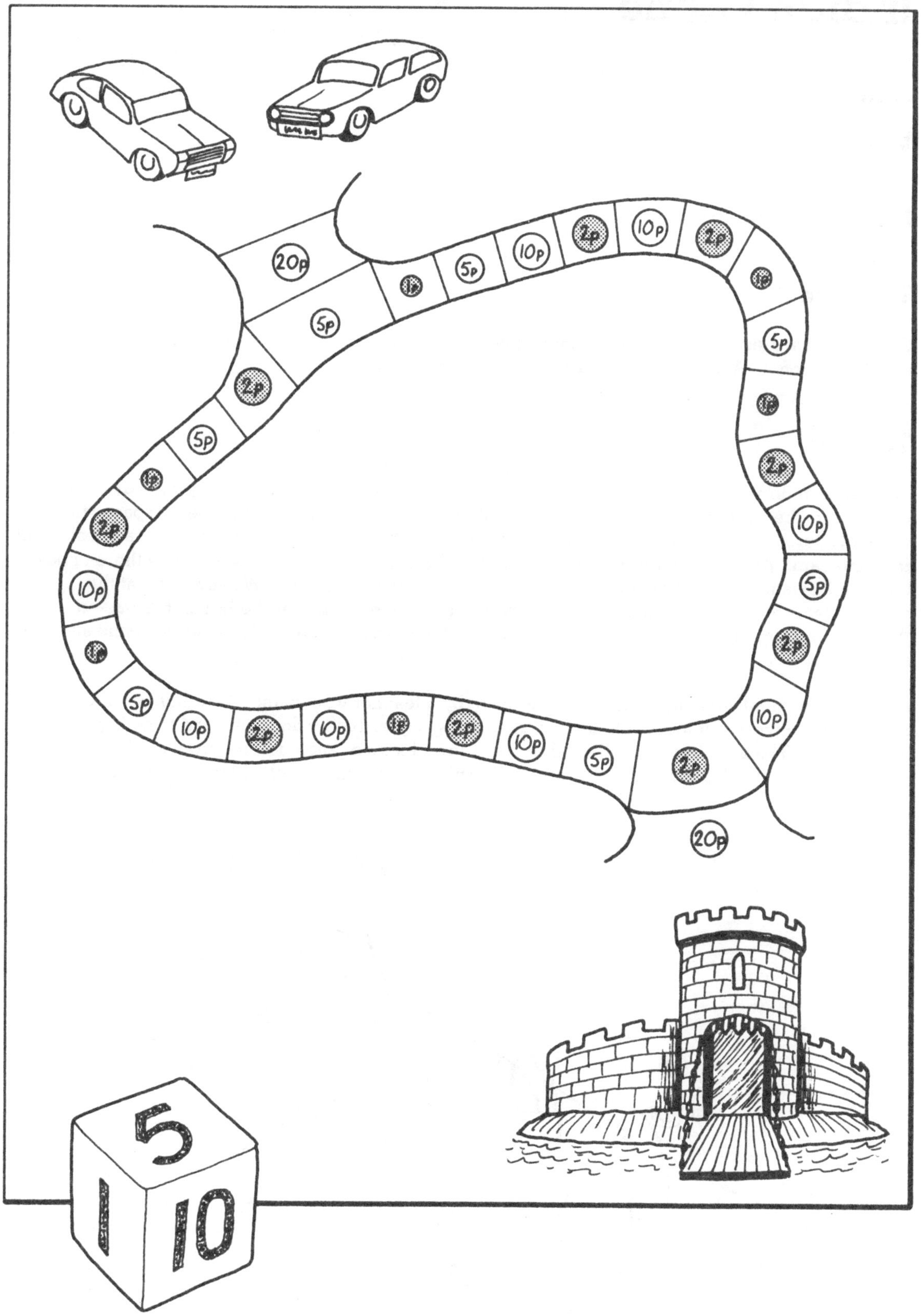
20p
5p
2p
5p
1p
2p
10p
1p
5p
10p
2p
10p
1p
2p
10p
5p
2p
1p
5p
10p
2p
10p
2p
1p
5p
1p
2p
10p
5p
2p
10p
20p
5
1
10

Indian Game

Aim

To give practice in addition.

Number of players 2 and a banker

To make

One base board size 51cm x 63.5cm as illustrated, two Indians for counters, two horses, and beads or rods for currency. A dice numbered 1-6 is also needed.

To play

The children throw the dice. The player with the lowest score begins. Players throw the dice and collect from the bank the amount shown on the dice. They then decide the number of spaces they can move through according to the number written in each space and how much they have collected from the bank. At the place where the track divides the player who is the first to arrive there chooses the path he wants to take. His opponent has to take the path which is left. We suggest that the children leave the correct number of beads by the side of the track after the Indian has passed through the area. This operation could indicate that the children have understood the game and are not cheating.

Note A delightful version of this game was made by a teacher who changed the Indians into robbers who were about to rob a house. Each space was guarded by dogs who had to be kept quiet with biscuits. The biscuits were collected by the throw of a dice. Each dog required a different number of biscuits. Real dog biscuits were used. The children only ate the black ones!

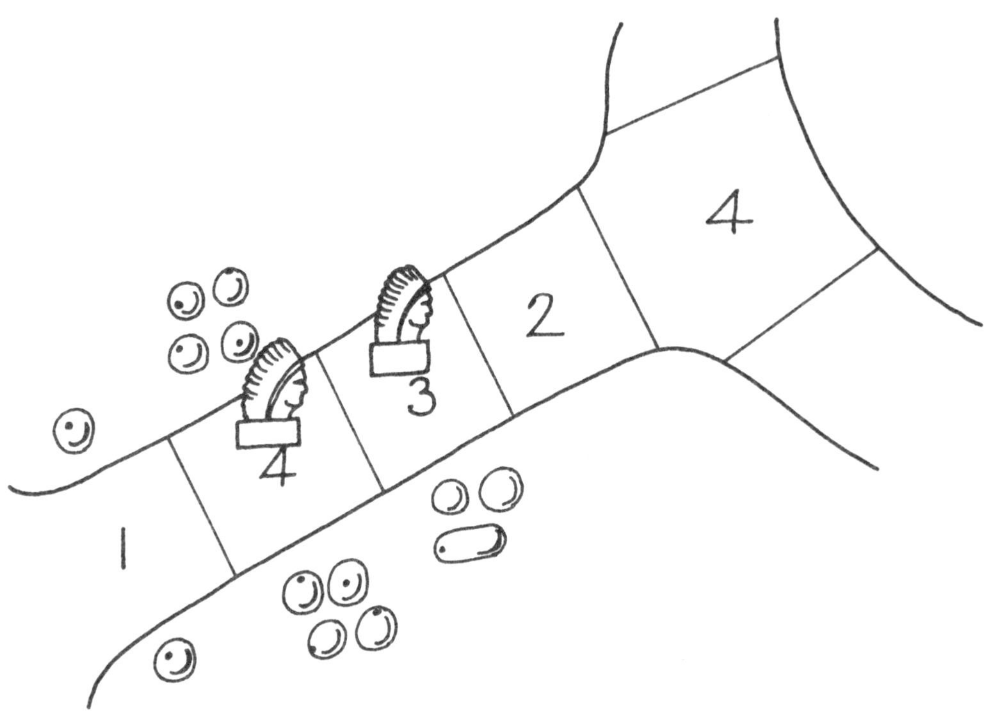

Perkin's Pot Luck

Aim

To give practice in multiplication.

Number of players 2 or more

To make

One base board, 51cm x 63.5cm as illustrated. The magic multiplication machines may be traced but the values must vary, e.g. 2 for every 1, 3 for every 1, 3 for every 2, etc. Make sure there is a machine on the last number. You will also need a dice numbered 1-6, two counters and real money may be used.

To play

Each player takes 1p from the bank and place their counters on the board. They then throw the dice. The player with the highest score begins. The players move along the track according to the number thrown on the dice. If they land on a machine then the player puts what money he has in the machine and takes out (from the bank) what the machine says has to come out, e.g. 2 for every 1. Both players race to the end of the track. The winner is the player with the most money.

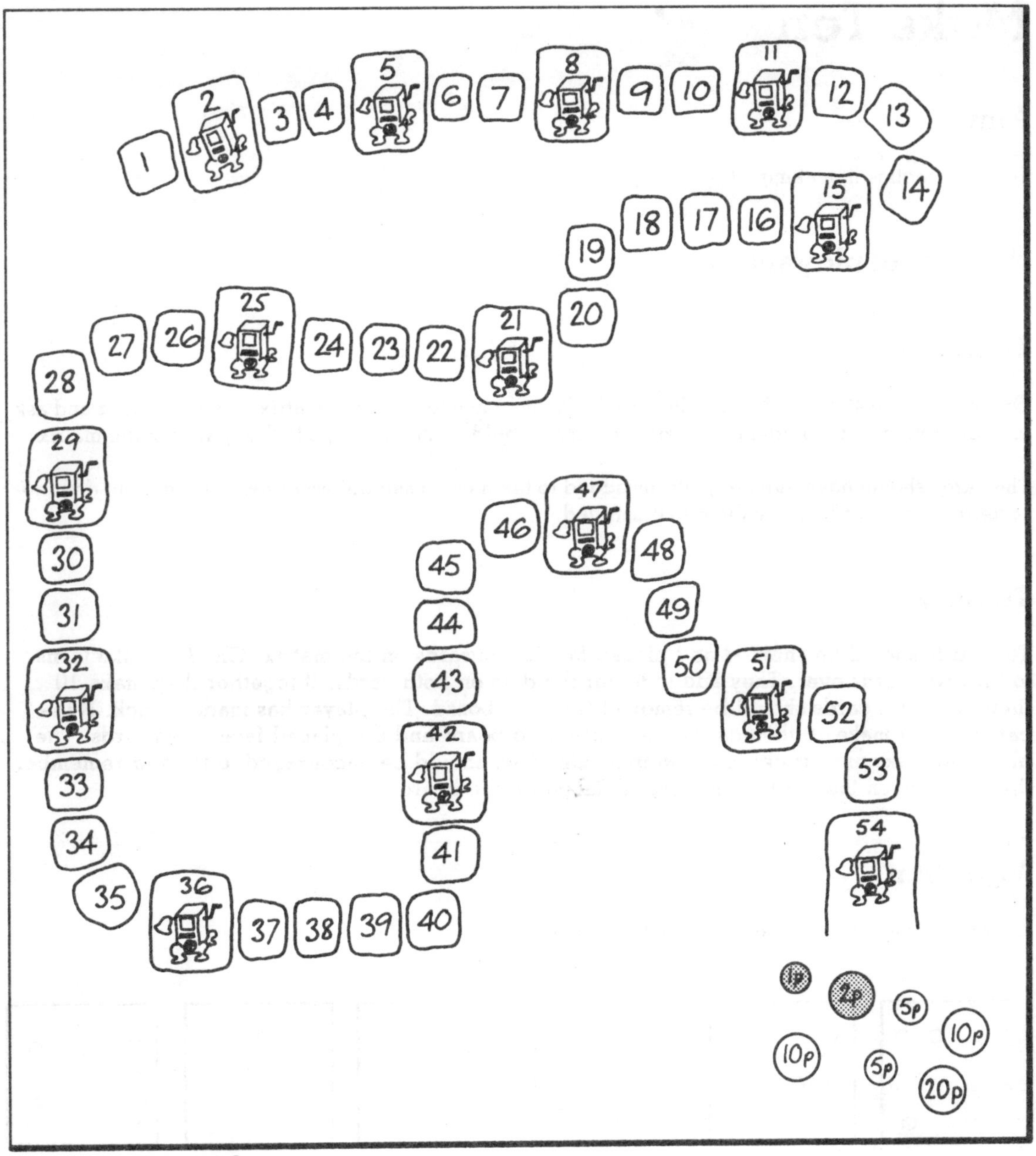
1
2
3
4
5
6
7
8
9
10
11
12
13
14
15
16
17
18
19
20
21
22
23
24
25
26
27
28
29
30
31
32
33
34
35
36
37
38
39
40
41
42
43
44
45
46
47
48
49
50
51
52
53
54
1p
2p
5p
10p
10p
5p
20p

2
1
3

Make Ten

Aim

To give practice in making 10.

Number of players 2

To make

One base board 47cm x 32cm as illustrated. You may like to make the matrix slightly smaller and ask the children to add a border of flowers. 18 cards should be made to fit into the spaces of the matrix.

The cards should have number patterns added to them using self-adhesive spots. Do not put domino patterns on the cards, make them as illustrated.

To play

The cards should be shuffled and placed face downwards on the matrix. Children take turns to turn two cards over. They add together the dots on both cards. If together they make 10 then those two cards should be removed from the board. The player has made a trick. If the cards do not make 10 then cards are returned to board and are placed face downwards. The player to make most tricks is the winner. Children should be encouraged to try and remember the numbers on the cards which are replaced on the board.

Variation

Other cards and boards can be made for 7, 8 and 9.

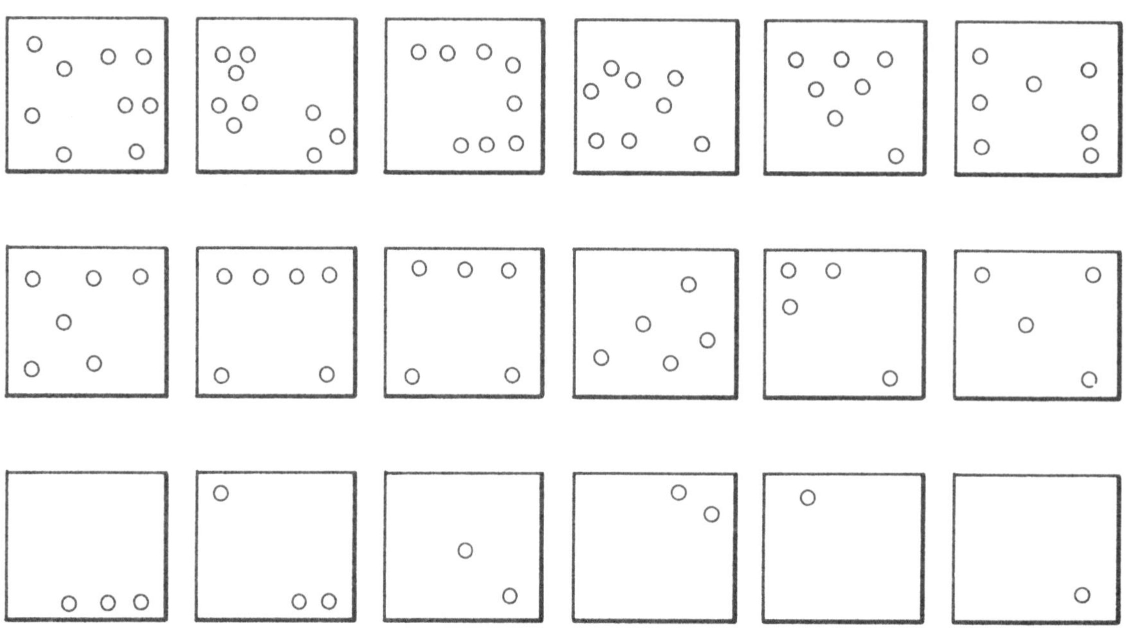

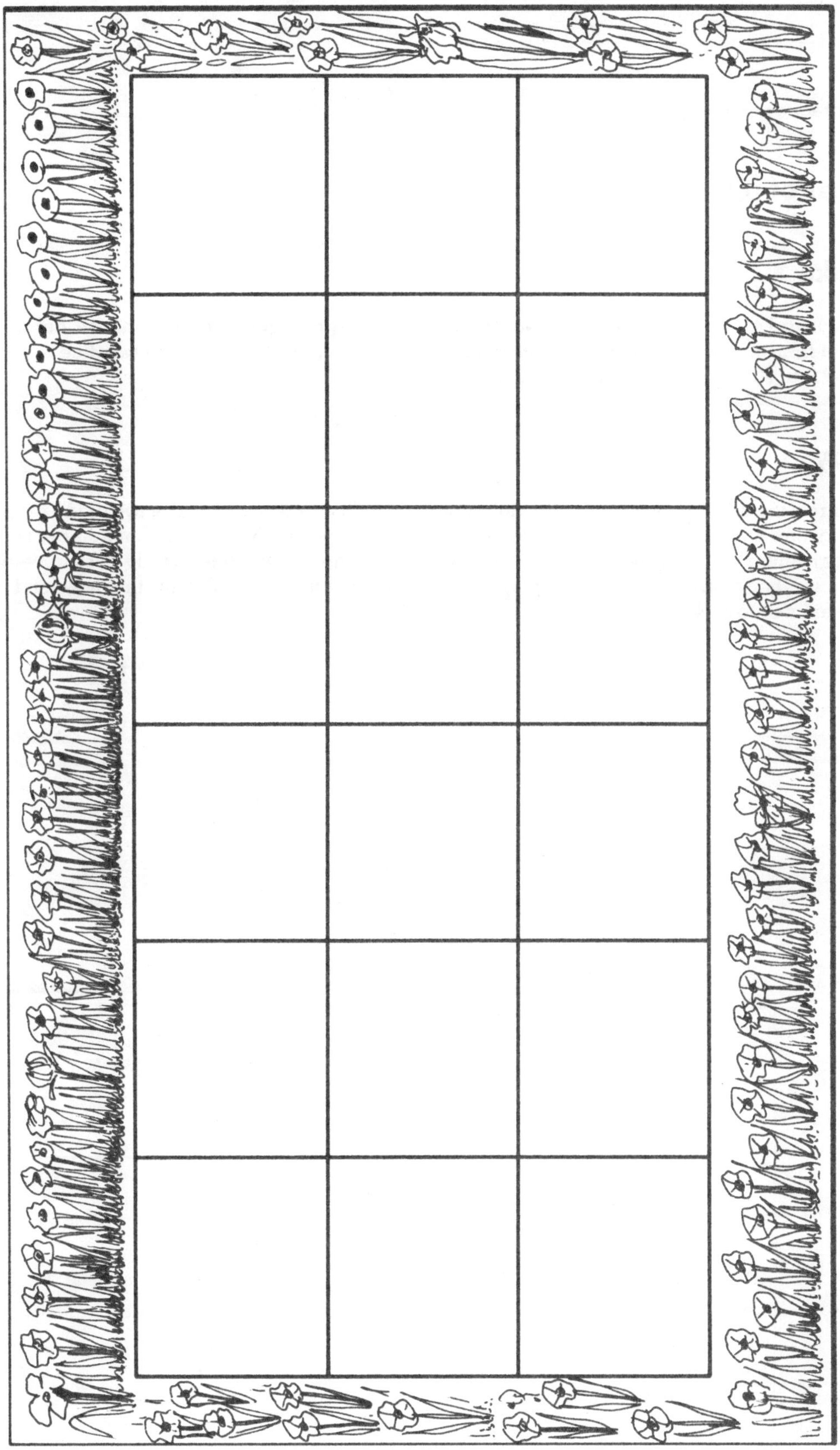

Save the Wildlife

Aim

To give practice in multiplication.

Number of players 2

To make

One base board 47cm x 32cm as illustrated. We used gift wrapping paper for the animals but they can be cut from old library books. Each animal has a number on it. You also need two dice numbered 1-6, 20 red counters and 20 green counters.

To play

Players throw the dice to see who has the highest number. That player starts. The two dice are thrown together and the two numbers shown are multiplied together. 3 x 2 = 6. That number is found on an animal and covered with one of his counters. If the number has already been covered by a counter, then a turn is missed. The players who can cover most animals wins the game and takes the animals to a Game Park.

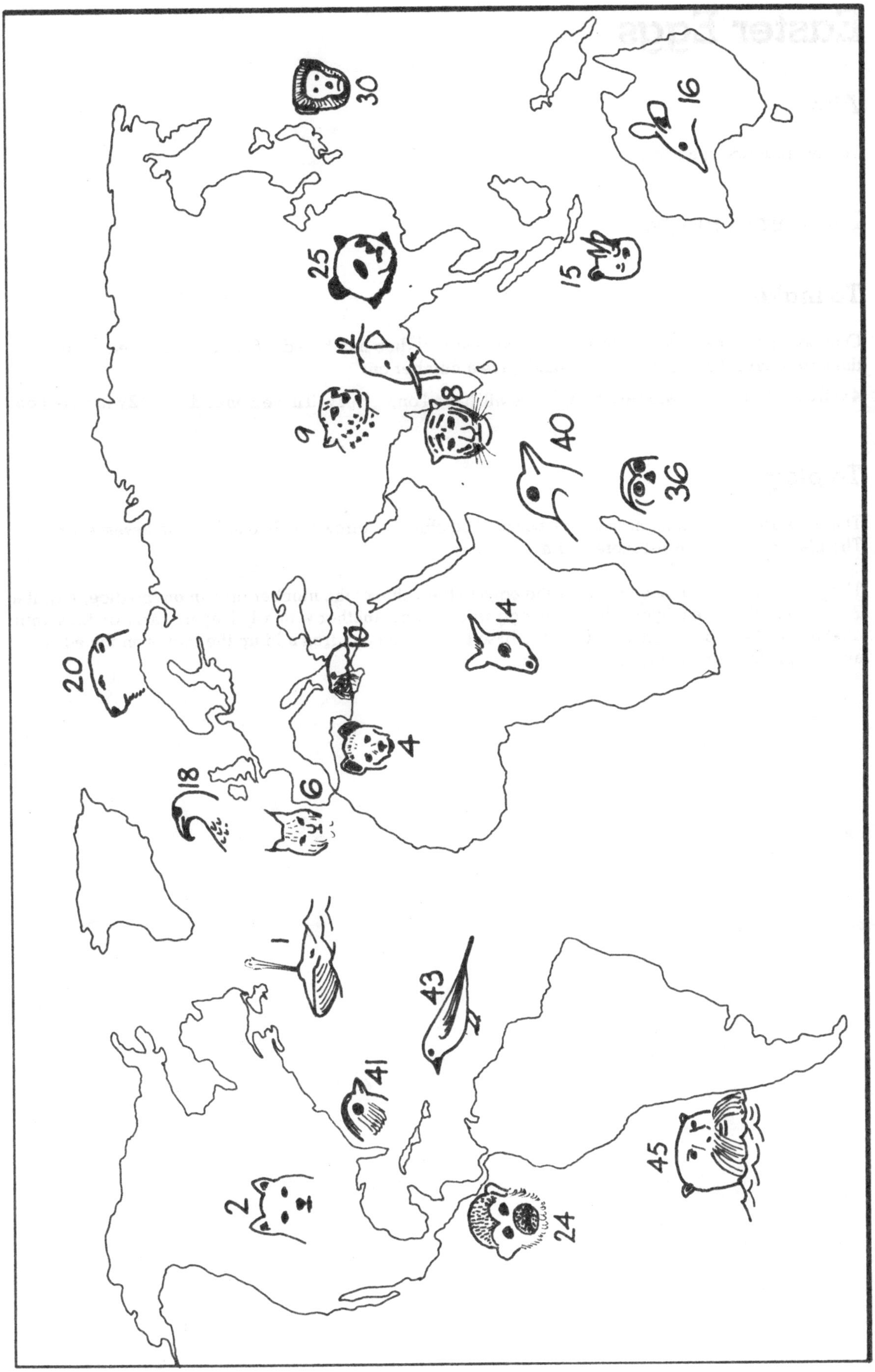
30
16
25
15
12
11
9
8
40
36
20
14
10
4
18
6
1
43
41
2
45
24

Easter Eggs

Aim

To give practice in addition.

Number of players 2

To make

One board 47cm x 32cm as illustrated, a commercial dice numbered 1-6 and copies of each egg on the base board. Each of the eggs should have a number on:

4 will have 8 on, 4 will have 6 on, 4 will have 4 on, 4 will have 2 on and 12 will have 1 on.

To play

The eggs are matched to those on the board. The children throw the dice to find the lowest score. The player with the lowest score begins.

The player throws the dice and takes the eggs to the value of the number thrown on the dice, e.g. if a 7 is thrown, then the player will take an egg with a 6 and another with a 1. Players carry on thus until all the eggs have been removed from the base board. The children add up the scores on the eggs and the player with the highest score wins.

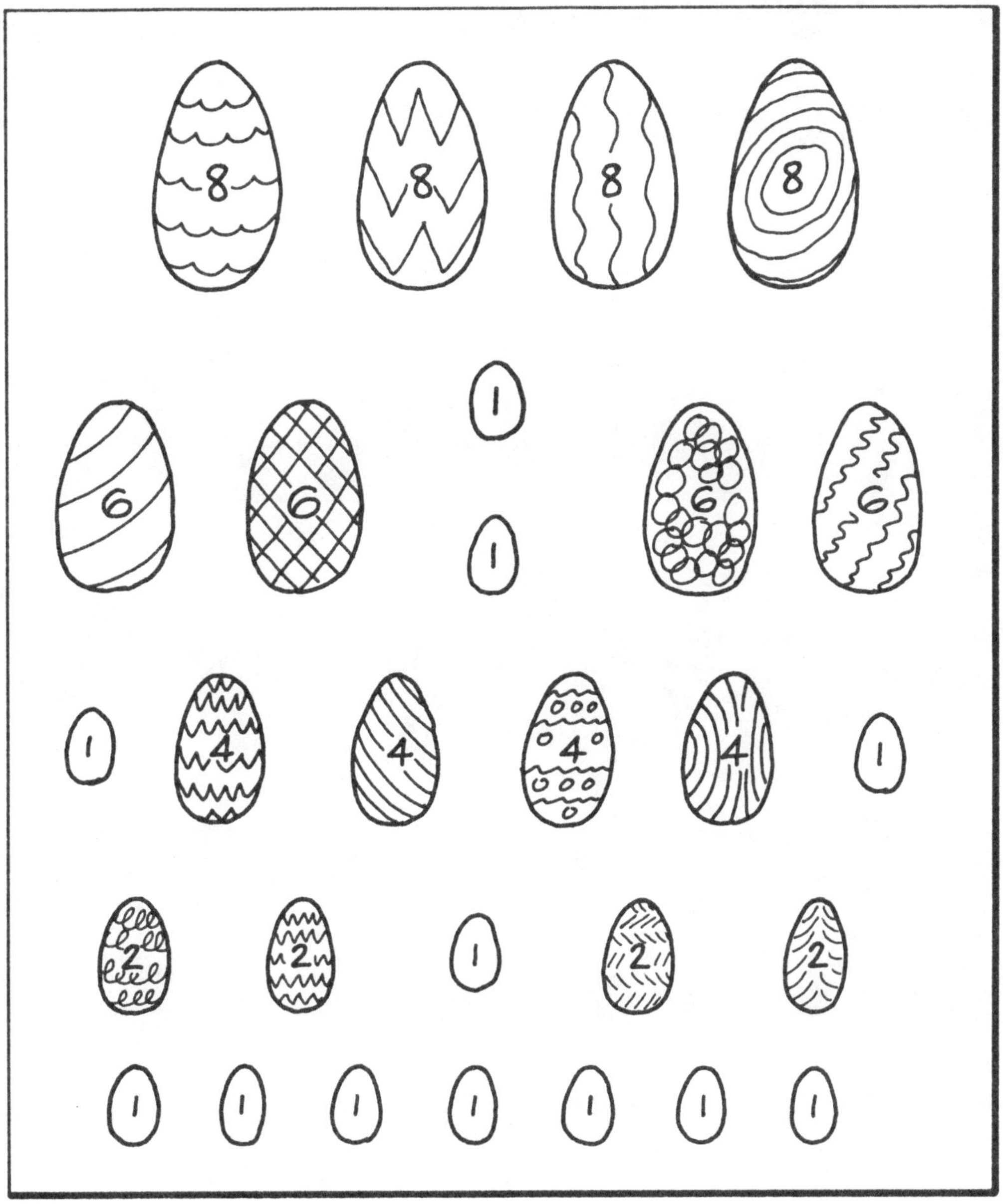
8
8
8
8
6
6
1
1
6
6
1
4
4
4
4
1
2
2
1
2
2
1
1
1
1
1
1
1

1
2
4

Games for the slow attainer

Games used as remediation tools for the older slow attainer should look more grown up than those previously described and we suggest that the classroom teacher looks at games which have been on the commercial market for many years as sources of inspiration. The teacher may like to look more closely at these games and try and deduce just what mathematical concepts are needed in order to play the game with success. If a child needs extra practice with addition, which games would give him that practice, or, if the rules were altered slightly, would enhance that practice? Similarly subtraction and multiplication could be dealt with.

Listed below are games which may be adapted for the classroom. The section which follows the list shows some alternative versions of well-known games which we have either seen in use in the classroom or have adapted ourselves:

Bagatelle
Beetle
Bingo
Chess
Draughts
Hex
Dominoes — Fives and Threes — Matador
Mancala
Ludo
Monopoly
Nim
Nine Men's Morris
Patience
Pelmanism
Rummy
Reversi
Royal Game of Goose
Skittles
Snakes and Ladders
Snap
Sprouts

Contents

Snakes and Ladders — 1

Aim

To give practice in addition.

Number of players 2 or more

To make

One base board 43.5cm x 51cm as illustrated. Note that the numbers in each decade are placed at random rather than in the usual order and that 0 is in the first decade. A dice numbered 1-6 and two or more counters are also needed.

To play

Each player in turn throws the dice and finds that number in the first throw. The second throw is added to the first and the player has then to find that number (moves cannot be made by counting on). Anyone throwing a six has another turn. If a player lands at the bottom of a ladder he climbs to the top; if he lands on the head of a snake he must move down to the bottom of the tail. Players must throw the exact number to finish.

Snakes and Ladders — 2

A similar version of the game can be made for subtraction where the players start at 100 and subtract their throws from the total. In this game the ladders and snakes must go the other way.

Snakes and Ladders — 3

A game to give practice in doubling and halving. This version can be played on a commercial board. When a player throws an odd number then that number is doubled and when an even number is thrown then that number is halved. Players move according to the new score.

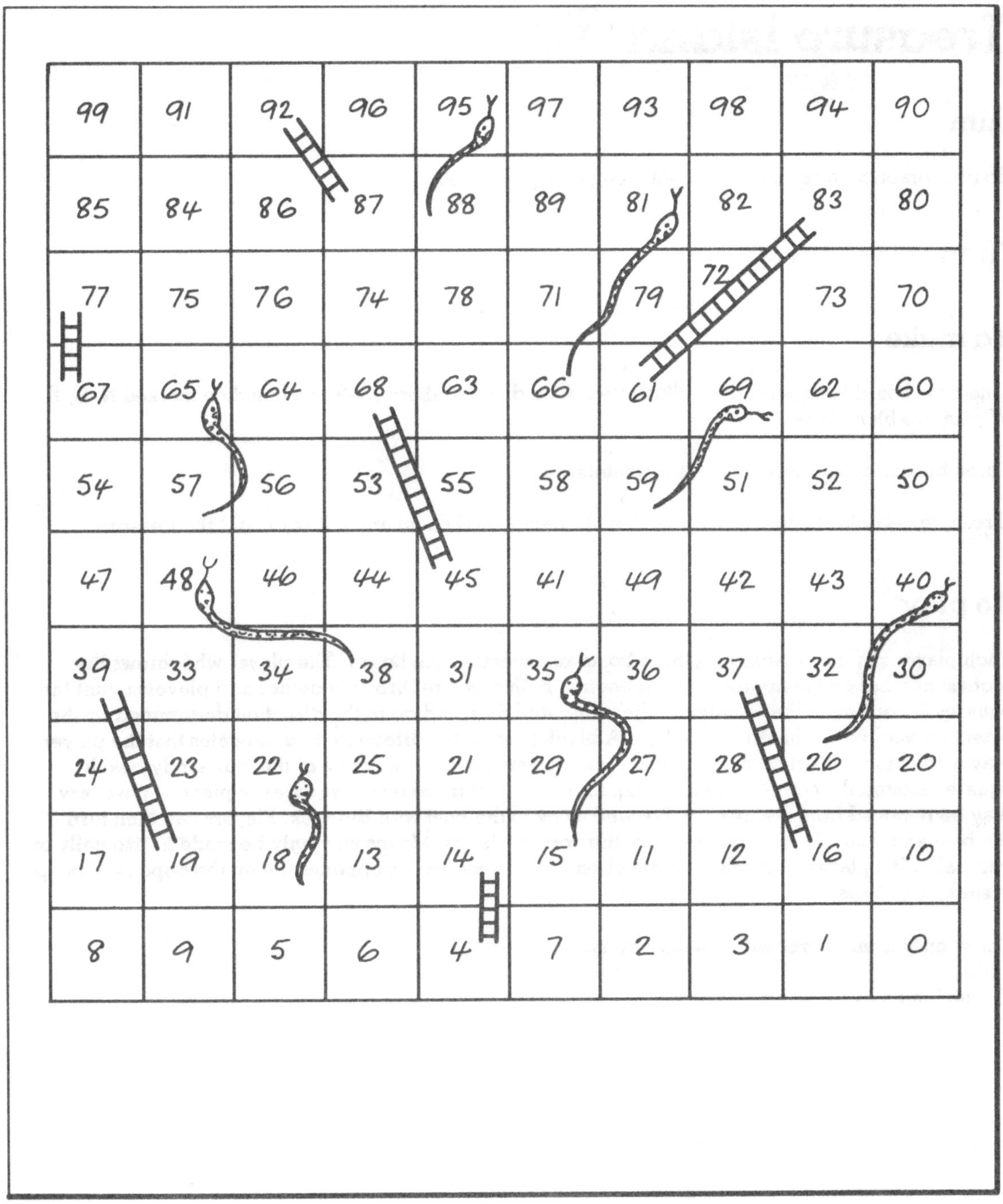
99 91 92 96 95 97 93 98 94 90
85 84 86 87 88 89 81 82 83 80
77 75 76 74 78 71 79 72 73 70
67 65 64 68 63 66 61 69 62 60
54 57 56 53 55 58 59 51 52 50
47 48 46 44 45 41 49 42 43 40
39 33 34 38 31 35 36 37 32 30
24 23 22 25 21 29 27 28 26 20
17 19 18 13 14 15 11 12 16 10
8 9 5 6 4 7 2 3 1 0

2
1
3

Treasure Island

Aim

To give practice in counting on, estimating and prediction.

Number of players 2

To make

One base board 50cm square, as illustrated. One dice numbered 1-6 and one dice marked **N, S, E, W** with two blank faces.

Three blue ships and three red ships (counters).

'Treasure' — gold (buttons), silver (buttons), diamonds (beads) and a box to hold the treasure.

To play

Each player starts by placing his three boats anywhere on the board. The player who throws the highest number on the numbered dice begins. Both dice are thrown together and players count the squares according to the number on the numbered dice and go in the direction determined by the direction marked on the direction dice. A blank face on the direction dice indicates that the player may move in the direction of his own choice. Players make for any one of the four sandy beach squares around the centre island. On landing on one of these beach squares, a piece of jewellery may be removed from the treasure box and stuck to the boat with Blu-tack. Players can then turn the boat and take it 'home' to any one of the corner islands. Moves may only be made horizontally or vertically. If a player lands on a square already occupied by his opponent, then the opponent's ship is sunk, with treasure.

The winner is the player with the most treasure.

A time limit may be set for this game.

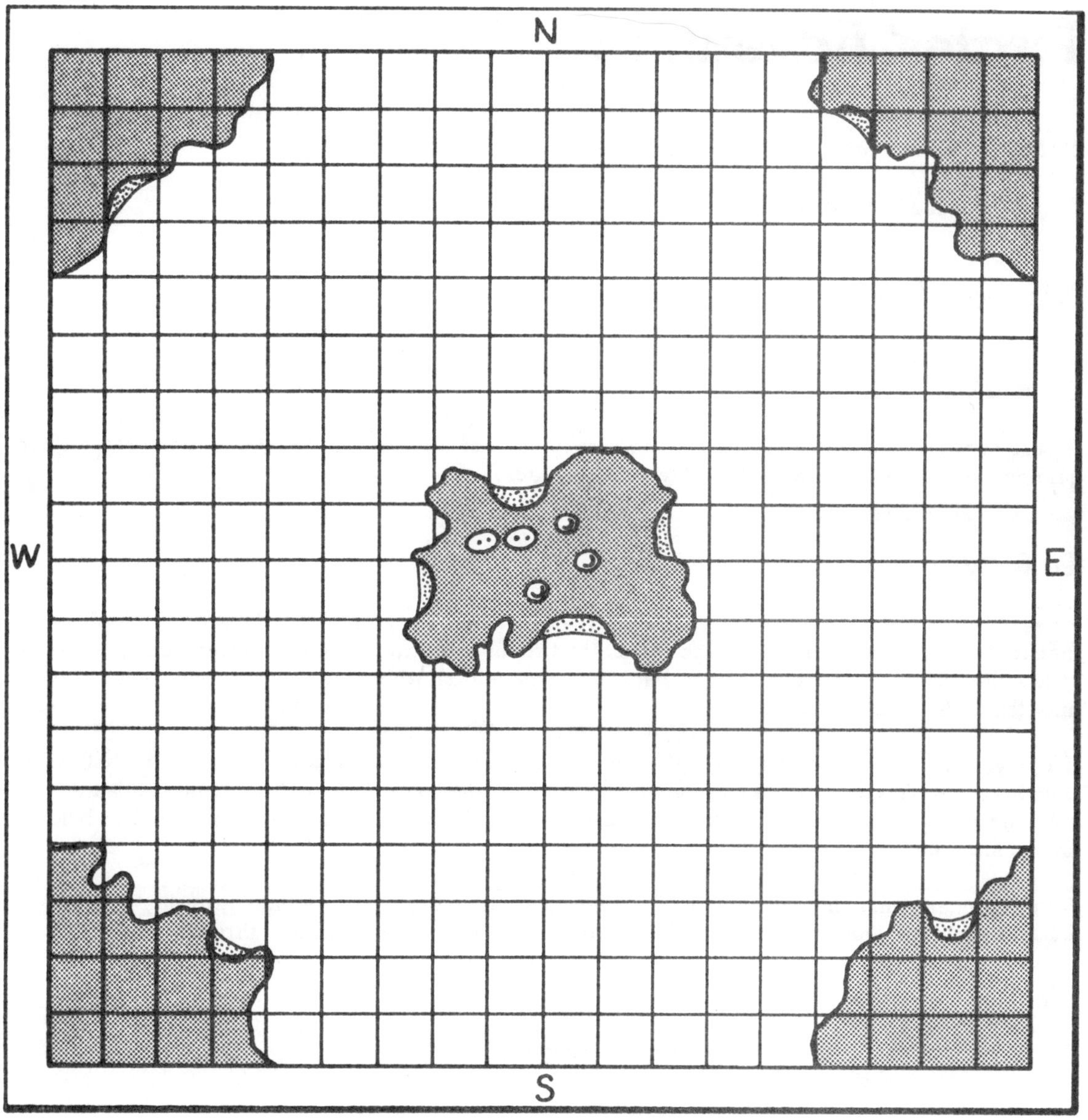
N
W
E
S

2
1
3
E
S

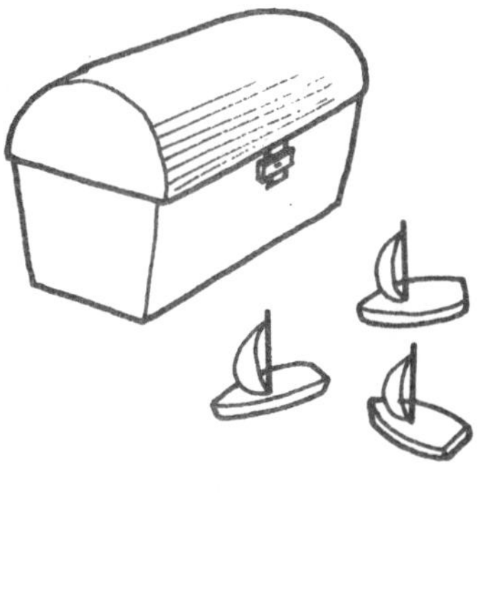

Pirates' Adventure

Aim

To give practice in addition and counting on.

Number of players 2 or more

To make

A base board similar to that illustrated, two dice numbered 1-6, a pirate counter for each player, five cannon cards, five treasure cards and five barrel cards.

To play

Players throw the dice to decide who shall start. They place their counters at the start. Each player then moves his counter forward by the sum of the two dice thrown. If two players land on the same space, the first pirate to arrive must go back to the space from which the second pirate came. Players must throw the exact amount to win.

If a player's pirate lands on a space with some cannon balls then the player takes a cannon ball card from the pack. This he may use later on his travels if he lands on a cannon. Should he reach a cannon square and not have a cannon ball card then the player has to throw a 6 on both dice before he can move on.

A treasure card will enable the player who lands on a pirate to move on without throwing a 6.
A barrel card will enable the player who lands on a ship to move on without throwing 6.

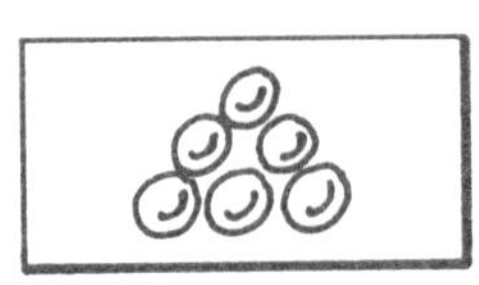

Cannon ball card

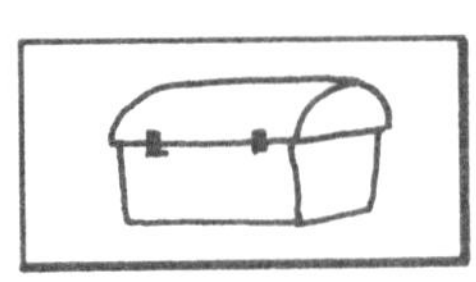

Treasure card

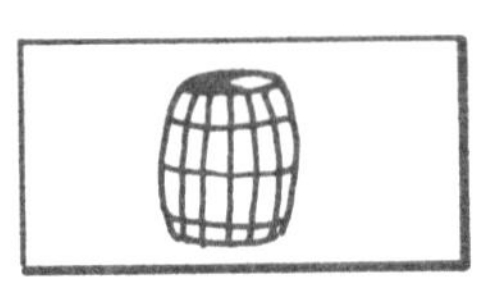

Barrel card

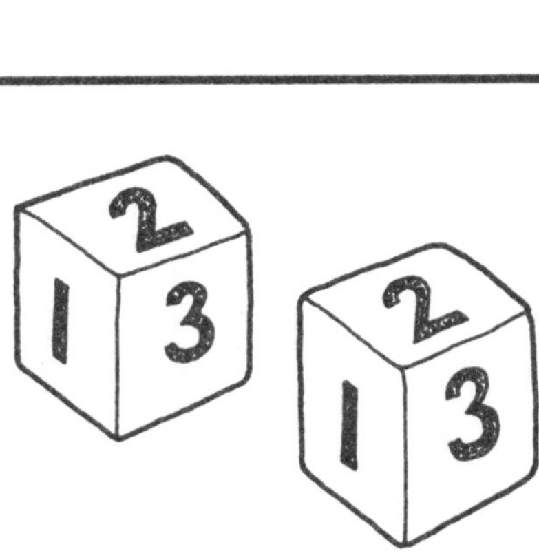
2
1
3
2
1
3

Pirates to the Island

Aim

To give practice in adding to 10 and counting in 10's.

Number of players 2

To make

A pirate board 29.5cm x 80cm, 2 pirate boats and

5 pirate cards with 1 pirate on,
5 pirate cards with 2 pirates on,
5 pirate cards with 3 pirates on,
5 pirate cards with 4 pirates on,
5 pirate cards with 5 pirates on,
5 pirate cards with 6 pirates on,
5 pirate cards with 7 pirates on,
5 pirate cards with 8 pirates on,
5 pirate cards with 9 pirates on.

To play

Place the pirate cards between the players who take turns to remove the top card from the pack of pirate cards. When a player has collected from the pack two cards which together have ten pirates then these two cards are placed on the base board, and the player's boat put on top of the two cards. The remaining cards are returned to the bottom of the pack of cards. Players continue thus, taking cards from the pile to make ten and putting them on the base board in sequence, until 100 is reached when that player will have won the game.

This game is really an addition and grouping game which should lead a child to the awareness of the tenness of ten and the understanding that 10 tens make 100.

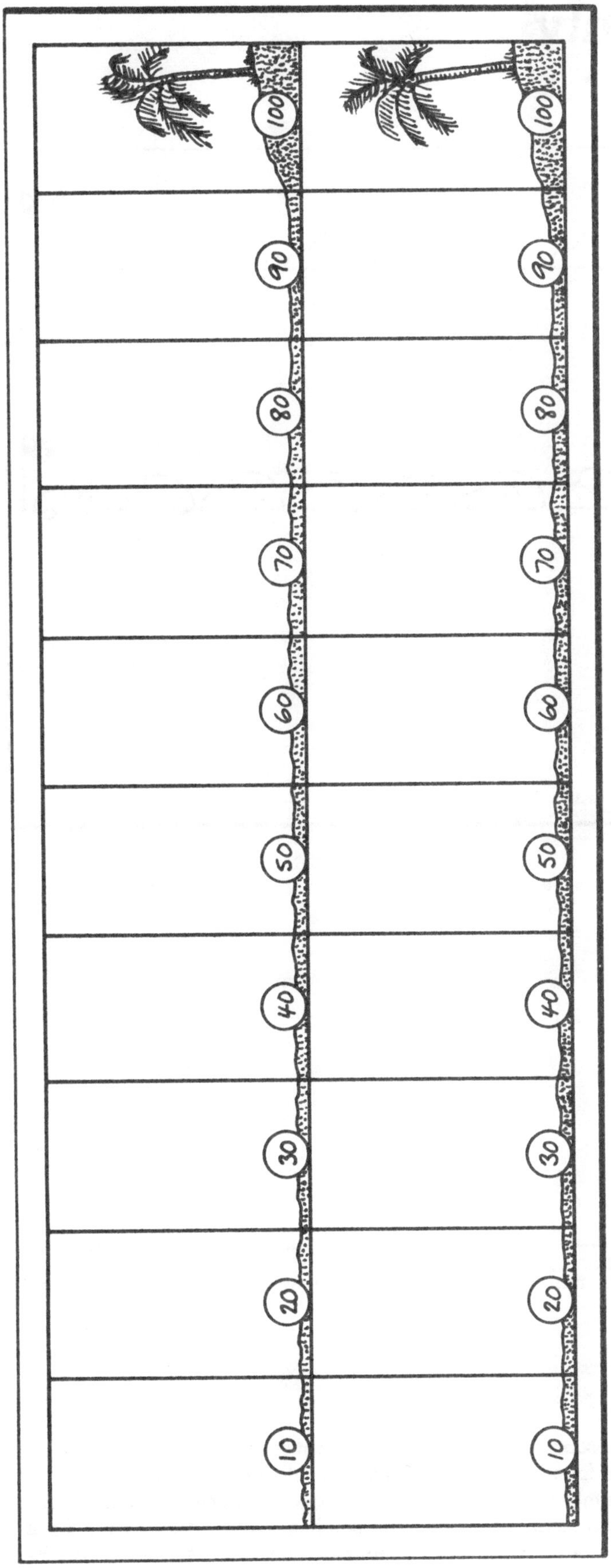
100
90
80
70
60
50
40
30
20
10
100
90
80
70
60
50
40
30
20
10

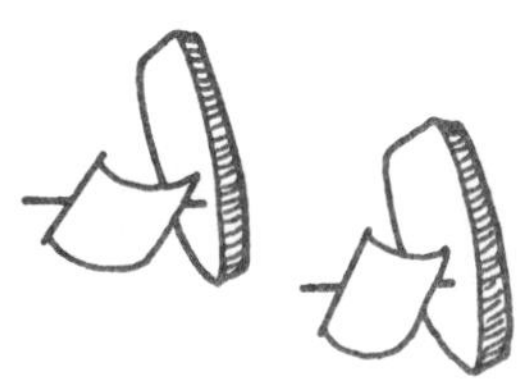

Silverstone Twenty

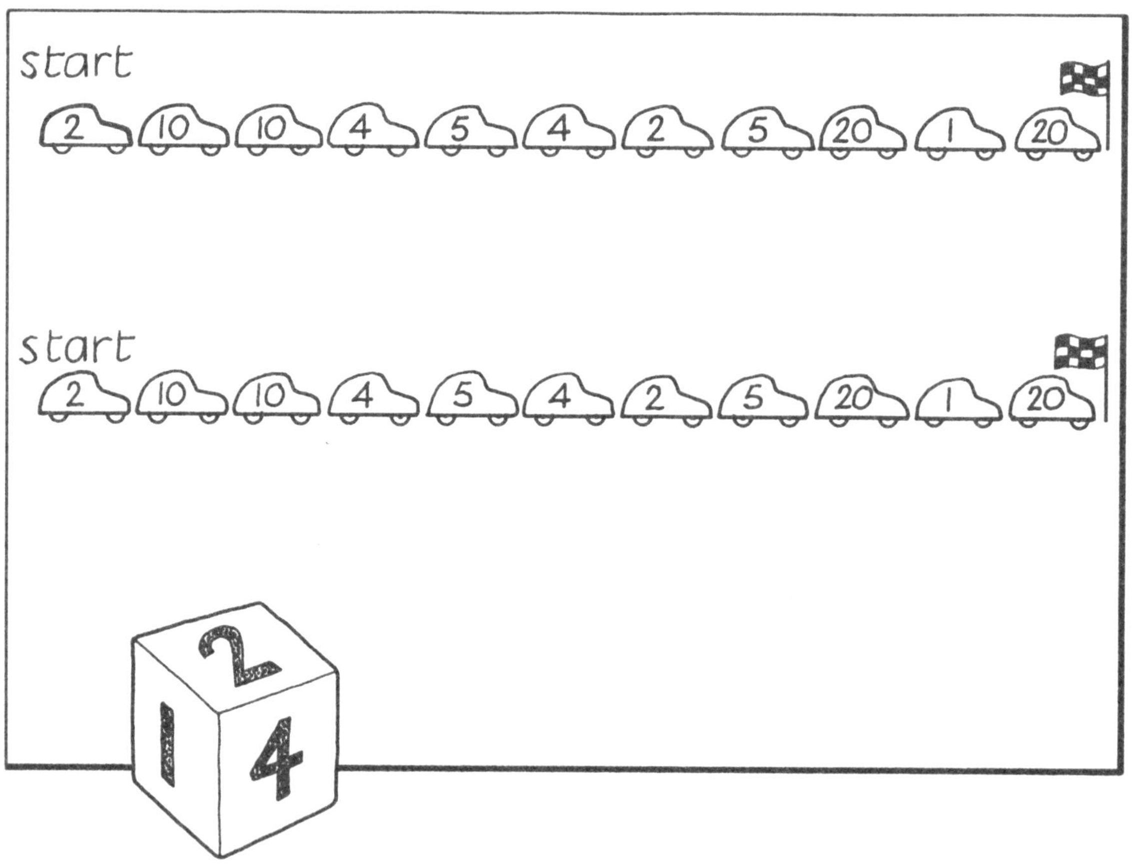

Aim

To give practice in division.

Number of players 2

To make

A board 47cm x 32cm as illustrated, a dice numbered with 1, 2, 4, 5, 10 and 20, 11 red counters and 11 yellow counters.

To play

Children choose counters and the highest score begins. The dice is thrown and the number on the dice is divided into 20. The answer is then found on a car and covered with a counter, e.g. if 20 is thrown, there is one 20 in 20, therefore number 1 on a car should be covered. Players take turns in throwing the dice and covering factors with counters until one person has covered all the cars. He is deemed the winner. If a player finds he has already covered a number, then he must miss a turn. 30 and 60 could be dealt with in this way.

Sweets!

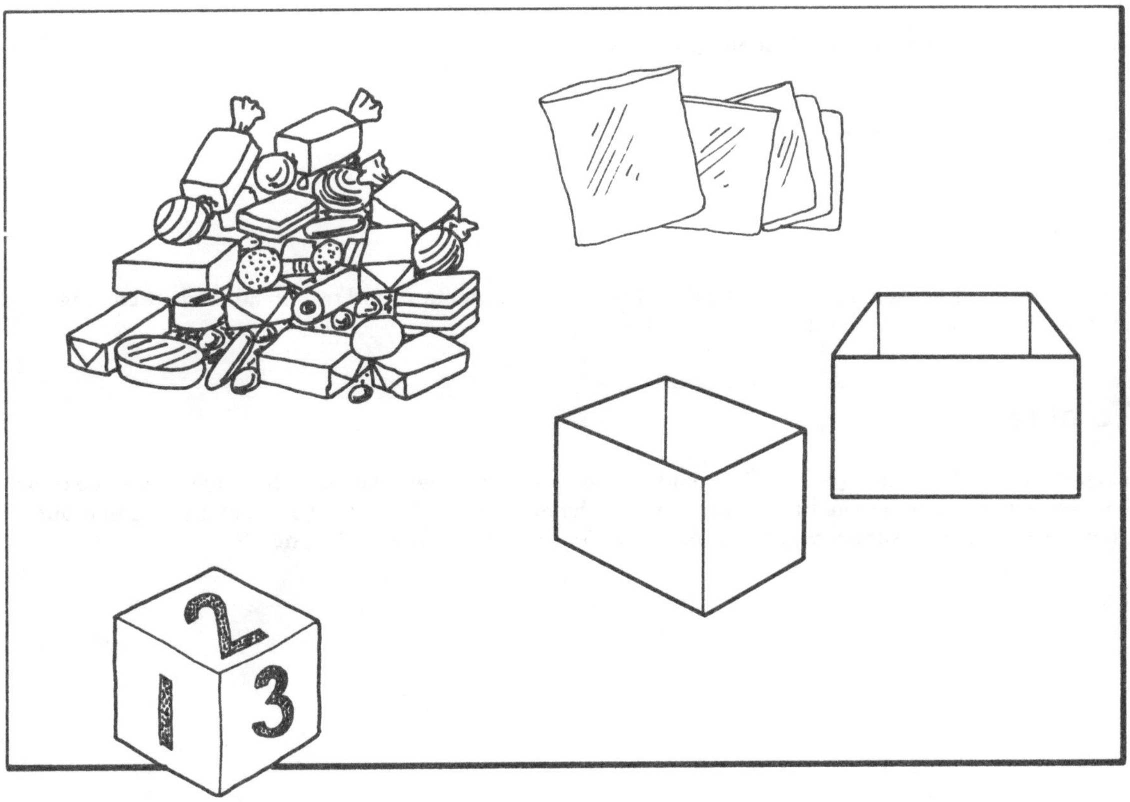

Aim

To give practice in bundling in 1 s and 10 s to make 100.

Number of players 2

To make

A large box of counters (for sweets) or pretend sweets made from a salt/flour dough, twenty polythene bags, two boxes and a commercial 1-6 dice.

To play

Players throw the dice and the player with the highest score begins. The children collect from the 'shop' the number of sweets as determined by the throw on the dice. As soon as ten sweets have been collected they should be put in a polythene bag. Players continue to collect sweets, putting them in bags as soon as they have collected ten in number. When a player has ten polythene bags, they are put in the box and that player is declared the winner.

Race to the Moon

Aim

To give practice in quick recall of number facts of the teen numbers.

Number of players 2

To make

One base board 47cm x 32cm as illustrated, two coloured counters and two home made dice, one marked 5, 6, 7, 8, 9, 10 and the other 6, 7, 8, 9, 10, 10.

To play

Players throw both dice together. They add together both numbers shown on the dice and move their counter to that number. The first player to reach the moon wins. This is not a counting on game but moves are made in a similar way to the moves in *Jumping Frogs* (pages **58 and 59**).

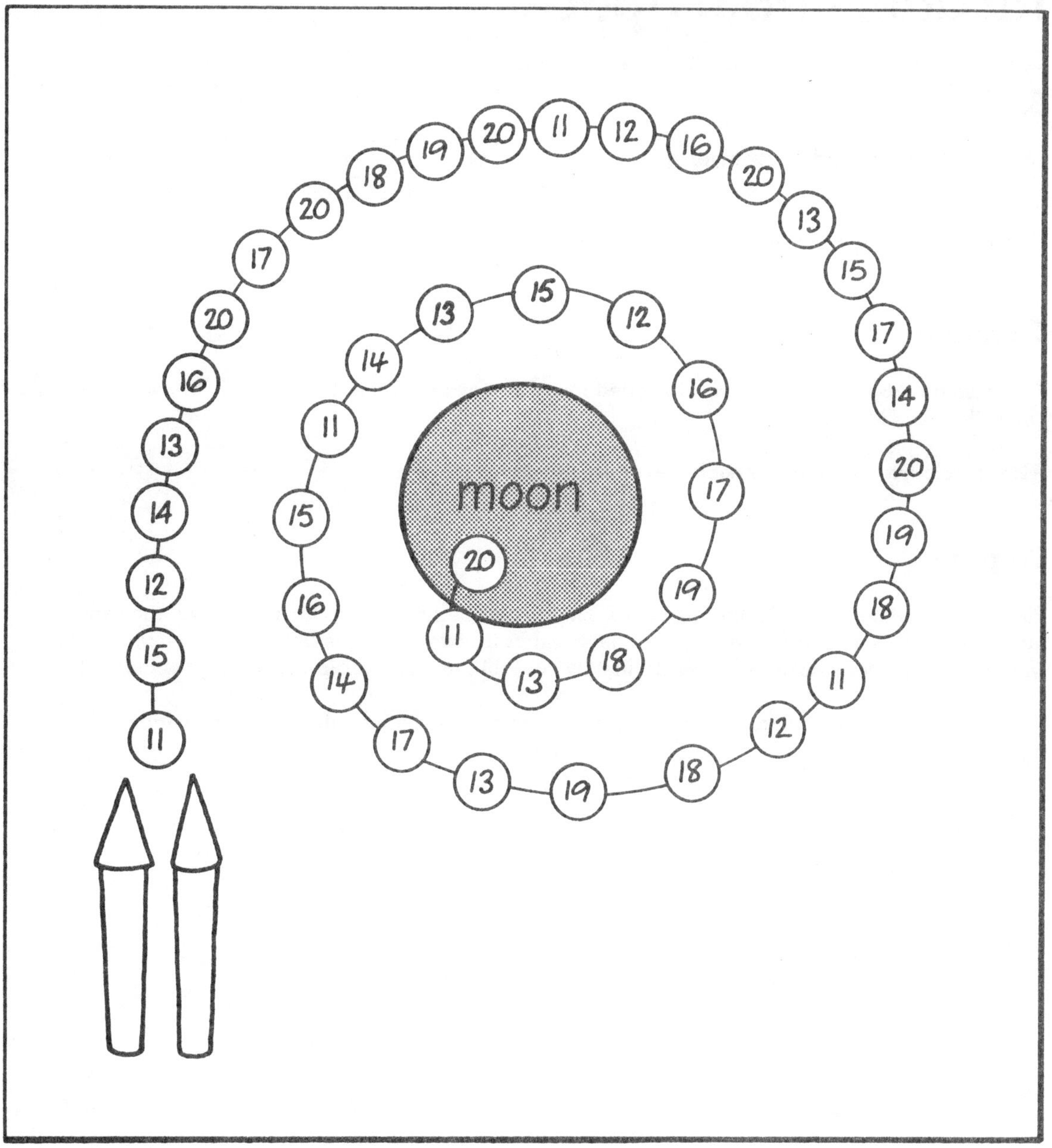
11
15
12
14
13
16
20
17
20
18
19
20
11
12
16
20
13
15
17
14
20
19
18
11
12
18
19
13
17
14
16
15
11
14
13
15
12
16
17
19
18
13
11
20
moon

7
6
5
8
6
7

Invaders from Space

Aim

To give practice in adding together 10's.

Number of players 2

To make

Two base boards, 47cm x 32cm as illustrated, two dice, one numbered with 10, 20, 30, 40, 50, 60 and one with 0, 10, 20, 30, 40, 50.

Also 15 coloured counters for each player are needed.

To play

Players throw dice to find the highest score. That player begins. Both dice are thrown, the two numbers shown are added together, and that number is covered on the board with a counter. The winner is the player who saves his world first by covering all his invading spaceships with counters.

This is only an elaborate game of Lotto, but sufficiently interesting to give practice in adding 10's together.

10
40
50
70
20
80
30
60
90
100
earth
50
70
60

20
0
10
30
10
20

Commercial games

Take two Frank Tapson (A & C Black)

The St Michael Book of Games Richard Sharp and John Piggott (eds) (St Michael)

Children play mathematics Z. P. Dienes and M. Holt (Piccolo)

Board and Table Games from Many Civilisations R. C. Bell (OUP)

Maths Games and Activities Roy Hollands (Hart Davis)

Fun with Maths Michael Holt (Piccolo)

Cassell Number Games Peter Avis (Cassell)